Backgammon
FOR
DUMMIES®

by Chris Bray

WILEY

A John Wiley and Sons, Ltd, Publication

Backgammon For Dummies®

Published by
John Wiley & Sons, Ltd
The Atrium
Southern Gate
Chichester
West Sussex
PO19 8SQ
England

E-mail (for orders and customer service enquires): cs-books@wiley.co.uk

Visit our Home Page on www.wiley.com

Copyright © 2009 John Wiley & Sons, Ltd, Chichester, West Sussex, England

Published by John Wiley & Sons, Ltd, Chichester, West Sussex

For general information on our other products and services, please contact our Customer Care Department within the U.S. at 800-762-2974, outside the U.S. at 317-572-3993, or fax 317-572-4002.

For technical support, please visit www.wiley.com/techsupport.

Wiley also publishes its books in a variety of electronic formats. Some content that appears in print may not be available in electronic books.

British Library Cataloguing in Publication Data: A catalogue record for this book is available from the British Library

ISBN: 978-0-470-77085-6

10 9 8 7 6 5 4 3

MIX
Paper from
responsible sources
FSC® C013604

About the Author

Chris Bray has been playing backgammon for over thirty years. He is a multiple tournament winner and plays regularly on the European circuit. Chris writes the only backgammon column published in a national newspaper, *The Independent*, where his words have graced many a breakfast table on a Saturday morning for the last fifteen years.

Chris is also a prolific author and *Backgammon For Dummies* is his fifth book. His other works include *What Colour is the Wind?* and *Second Wind*.

Chris lives in south-west London with his wife Gill and daughter Kate.

Author's Acknowledgements

Firstly I would like to thank all at Wiley who have been involved with this book and given me help and guidance along the way. The backgammon community has complained for years that having no *For Dummies* book was a serious omission. I am pleased to say that oversight has now been corrected.

I would like to thank my technical reviewer, Ray Kershaw, for the accuracy of his work and his helpful insights.

Finally, I would like to thank my wife and daughter for their patience while this book was being written. Authors tend to write at strange times of day and I am no exception – I have often seen the dawn break as I wrote!

Dedication

For Gill and Kate.

Publisher's Acknowledgements

We're proud of this book; please send us your comments through our Dummies online registration form located at www.dummies.com/register/.

Some of the people who helped bring this book to market include the following:

Acquisitions, Editorial, and Media Development

Project Editor: Rachael Chilvers

Development Editor: Kathleen Dobie

Copy Editor: Kate O'Leary

Proofreader: Kim Vernon

Commissioning Editor: Wejdan Ismail

Technical Reviewer: Ray Kershaw

Publisher: Jason Dunne

Executive Project Editor: Daniel Mersey

Cover Photos: © John Lamb/Getty Images

Cartoons: Rich Tennant
 (www.the5thwave.com)

Composition Services

Project Coordinator: Lynsey Stanford

Layout and Graphics: Joni Burns, Carl Byers, Reuben W. Davis

Proofreaders: Caitie Kelly

Indexer: Cheryl Duksta

Special Help

Brand Reviewer: Jennifer Bingham

Contents at a Glance

Table of Contents

Introduction

*T*hirty years ago I was an avid chess player. My girlfriend (now wife) taught me to play backgammon but I didn't take it seriously. Then one night I was working through the small hours testing some software (computers weren't quite as fast in the late 1970s as they are today) and a colleague challenged me to a game of backgammon while we waited for the electronic abacus to perform.

In 45 minutes I lost £10 and discovered that I knew absolutely nothing about the game. That really annoyed me and the next day I bought two books on backgammon. I read the books (more than once), practised with a friend, and a month later challenged my work colleague again. I recovered my £10 and won some more besides. Justice!

I've loved the game for 30 years now and play nearly every day, either live or on the Internet. Backgammon continues to fascinate and astound me and some of my closest friends have come from the world of backgammon. I hope the game gives you as much pleasure as it has given me.

About This Book

The ideal way to discover backgammon is to combine tuition and study with playing the game. I can't be your playing partner but I can pass on my knowledge to you for you to study and that's why I've taken so much pleasure in writing *Backgammon For Dummies*.

Over the years I've introduced a lot of people to backgammon by approaching the game in a relatively logical fashion but at the same time (hopefully) I've made it fun for my students. I hope this book comes across in the same way.

I cover every aspect of backgammon in this book, so if you're a novice you'll find sufficient information to get you acquainted with the game and able to play at a reasonable level. If you already know how to play, you'll find plenty of information to help you improve your game and gain a greater understanding of it.

Whether you're a complete beginner or an experienced player, I hope you'll find this book really useful in improving and enjoying your game.

Conventions Used in This Book

No, not backgammon conventions yet! (Although you can find where to play tournament backgammon in Chapter 16.) The conventions I use enable you to navigate this book as easily as possible.

I designate the two players Black and White and whenever I ask you to assess a position or calculate a play, you'll be playing as Black.

I alternate between male and female pronouns in odd and even chapters to be fair to both genders. So White swaps between being male and female!

The action parts of numbered steps are in **bold** and web addresses are in monofont. When I introduce a new term, it appears in *italics*.

I include many illustrations of backgammon boards. You'll find explanations of these along the way.

Foolish Assumptions

I assume, perhaps wrongly, that you:

- ✔ Have never played a game of backgammon in your life.
- ✔ Are keen to discover a game that's fascinated humankind for 5,000 years and continues to baffle people despite help from computers.
- ✔ Aren't that accustomed to using dice.
- ✔ Aren't a maths genius when it comes to the arithmetic that's part of the game.

I hope that this book answers all your backgammon questions.

How This Book is Organised

The great thing about *For Dummies* books is that you don't have to read them all the way through. You can simply turn to the bit you want – a chapter, a section, even just a paragraph. The table of contents and the index can help you out. Of course, the various elements of backgammon are all linked to each other and I sometimes make reference to one chapter from another (mainly as a reminder) but in the main how you navigate is up to you.

Here's a taster of what lies ahead.

Part 1: Starting and Playing the Game

This part covers all the basics that you need to start playing backgammon. I start with how to set up the checkers on the board, and look at the basic rules of the game including the different ways of playing. I describe some of the very basic tactics you need to understand to enjoy playing the game. Finally in this part, I look at how to play the opening moves. Like many games, the first few moves in backgammon are crucial to later success.

Part 11: Handling the Middle Game

Part II is all about the complex area known as the middle game. The part starts with a couple of chapters on doubling, probably the most difficult area of the game and one that still causes arguments whenever players discuss the game. The rest of the part is devoted to handling all the possible types of middle game that can occur.

Part III: Bearing Off (The Last Lap)

After the opening and the middle game, the next logical step is the ending and Part III looks at how to bear the checkers off the board – the final stage in any game of backgammon. Apparently simple at first sight, I explore some hidden subtleties in this stage of the game.

Part IV: Varying the Play

Backgammon is a game that's infinite in its variety. Chapter 11 looks at complex endings. After that I explore the multi-person version of backgammon known as chouette, which is great fun to play and also great to pick up tips from. Finally I look at tournament play – the most difficult form of the game. In the last chapter, I give advice and guidance about venturing onto the Internet to play online.

Part V: The Part of Tens

Here, in a concise and information-packed part, you'll find my personal list of recommended books for further study, a list of useful backgammon resources, and my ten backgammon commandments. Perhaps not quite as strict as the original commandments, these help you to remember some of the key points from the book.

Icons Used in This Book

The icons in this book highlight particular points to remember, be cautious of, or take on board (no pun intended) to improve your game.

You'll find the doubling cube next to interesting backgammon facts and history – the lore that makes the game so fascinating.

Whenever I use a word or phrase specific to backgammon, I let you know with this icon.

I help you to get to grips with backgammon by including heaps of examples of games in progress.

This icon draws your attention to an important point to bear in mind.

The target symbol highlights tips to help you become a better player – always assuming you can put the hint to good use!

As in all games you have pitfalls to steer clear of. This symbol indicates something you need to avoid or at least give considerable thought to.

Where to Go from Here

Enough of the preamble. The time has come for you to start to play the greatest game in the world. If you're not sure where to begin, why not be logical and have a look at Chapter 1, which makes the necessary introductions, and starts you on the road to backgammon mastery?

Part I

Starting and Playing the Game

'The object of backgammon is to get all of your checkers on this side of the board without me screaming and tipping your chair into the pool.'

In this part . . .

I equip you to get started in playing backgammon, by knowing how to set up the board and the checkers, and the basic rules and tactics of the game, especially the opening moves.

Chapter 1

Tackling the Basics of Backgammon

*A*re you one of the thousands of people who have a backgammon board kicking around at home but have never actually played the game? Or perhaps you've played a couple of games with a friend or relative and had your interest whetted? Maybe you've played the game quite a bit and feel yourself to be invincible? Let me assure you that absolutely anybody can play backgammon and get many hours of enjoyment and mental stimulation from the game.

In this chapter, I define the game of backgammon and discuss the basics of how you play and the equipment you need.

Looking at the Basics of the Game

Backgammon is a board game in which players on two opposing sides use the roll of two dice each in a race to get 15 playing pieces around a board with 24 points, bear them off, and thus win the game.

The game requires at least two players, although variations, which I explain in Chapter 12, allow more than two players to take part.

At its simplest, backgammon is a racing game, but because the pieces of the two opposing sides come into conflict while racing, the strategy and tactics can become very subtle. So, although the objective of the game is very straightforward and can appear deceptively easy, the many dangers and obstacles the pieces encounter as they make their journey around the board provide the game with infinite variety and challenges.

You're awarded a different number of points for different ways of winning. I explain the types of wins in Chapter 2.

Setting Up the Board and Arranging the Pieces

Backgammon is played on a board consisting of 24 narrow triangles called *points*. The triangles alternate in colour and are grouped into four quadrants of six points each. The quadrants are referred to as the player's *home board* and *outer board* and the opponent's home board and outer board. Your home and outer boards are the quadrants nearest to you. A ridge down the centre of the board called the *bar* separates the home and outer boards from each other. Figure 1-1 shows a backgammon board with the four boards and the bar identified.

Backgammon boards typically come as little briefcases that fold out flat to create the board. This space-saving feature makes them easy to carry.

Each player has 15 pieces. Unlike chess, where the two players most commonly have white or black pieces, in backgammon the pieces – or stones or men or *checkers*, which is the term I prefer and use throughout the book – can be any two colours.

Figure 1-2 shows the starting position for both the player's and opponent's 15 checkers.

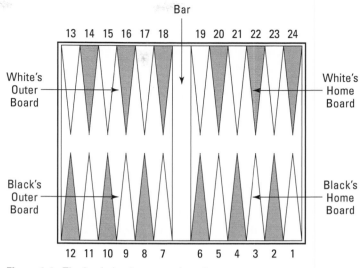

Figure 1-1: The basic backgammon board.

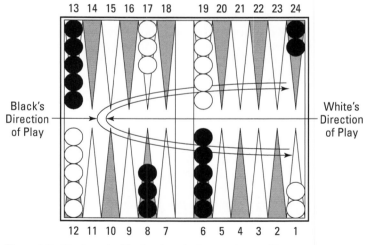

Figure 1-2: The board with checkers in the starting position.

On a real board the points aren't numbered, but I did it here so that I can refer to the points by number in the text.

Before starting the game, you place your checkers in their starting positions:

- ✔ Five checkers on your 6-point in your home board
- ✔ Three checkers on your 8-point in your outer board
- ✔ Five checkers on your 13-point in your opponent's outer board
- ✔ Two checkers on your 24-point in your opponent's home board.

Your opponent sets her checkers opposite to yours in a mirror image.

From your opponent's point of view, the point numbers are reversed. Your 13-point is your opponent's 12-point, your 3-point his 22-point, and so on.

You can set up the board with your home board on your right or left. If your home board is on your right-hand side, you move your checkers anticlockwise, as Black does in Figure 1-2. If your home board is to your left, you move in a clockwise direction, as White does in the illustration.

You may be more comfortable with one set-up or the other when you first start to play, but you soon get used to playing either way round. In the days before electricity, the board was always set up with the home boards nearest to the strongest source of light. In the twenty-first century, we no longer have that particular problem!

Examining the Rest of the Equipment

What else do you need other than the board and the checkers before you start to play? The following sections tell you.

Dice

In backgammon, the moves are determined by the roll of dice. Each player has two standard dice with six faces each bearing a number from 1 to 6. The dice are normally, but not always, the same colour as the checkers.

Opposite sides of a die always add up to seven, so the 6 faces the 1, the 4 faces the 3, and the 5 faces the 2.

In good quality backgammon boards, you find what are known as *precision dice*, the same as used in casinos. They're called precision dice because they're machined in such a way that each face of the die has an identical weight and so the die gives what is known as *true rolls*, which means that if you roll the die thousands of times, each of the six numbers land face up approximately the same number of times.

Dice shakers or dice cups

In backgammon, you're not allowed to throw the dice from your hand onto the board. Like the majority of games (other than craps) that involve dice, you must use a dice shaker to eliminate cheating. Amazingly, a good dice mechanic can cheat and roll a specific number if he's allowed to roll from his hand. Shakers eliminate this possibility.

A dice shaker is a cup (like a drink holder) normally made of leather or plastic. The best dice shakers have a slight ridge just below the lip on the inside so that the dice catch the ridge as they're projected onto the board and then they roll rather than slide. The shakers aren't always perfectly round because they need to fit into the board when the board is folded up.

Doubling cube

Finally, but most importantly, when you buy a backgammon board you find the doubling cube inside. This six-sided die is marked with the numbers 2, 4, 8, 16, 32, and 64, although you occasionally find a doubling cube marked with a 1 instead of a 64.

The doubling cube keeps track of the number of points at stake in each game as well as indicating which player last doubled. At the start of the game the doubling cube is set with the 64 face uppermost and is placed in the centre of the board and to one side.

I explain all about the doubling cube and how this cube is used in Chapter 6 but for now just remember this – of all the pieces of equipment, the doubling cube is by far the most difficult to master.

Digging into the Underlying Concepts

I'm often asked, 'What skills do I need to be good at backgammon?' The answer to that question gives you an idea of what lies ahead in this book.

Buying your own board

Literally thousands of backgammon boards are available from all sorts of retailers. No standard size or colour exists and so buying a board is very much a matter of personal style, taste, and, needless to say, budget.

The most expensive board I ever saw cost just a fraction under £2 million! Made of solid gold and inlaid with 60,000 tiny diamonds, I suppose its price was not unreasonable – but it was totally impractical to actually play on.

Back in the real world, you can buy a board for as little as £10 or as much as £2,000 or even more. I recommend buying a board of a reasonable size (very small boards strain the eyes); ideally about 45 centimetres by 28 centimetres when folded in half (nearly all backgammon boards fold in half for transportation). The colours of the checkers and the points I leave entirely to you. If you can afford them, I also encourage you to buy precision dice.

One final point is that I advise against a wooden board unless you want a very noisy game! I provide useful sources of equipment in Chapter 16.

Backgammon is known as a game of *total information*, meaning that you can see everything on the board in front of you, as you do when you play chess. Having total information is very different to *partial information* card games such as poker and bridge, in which you have to spend considerable time and mental energy trying to work out what cards your opponents hold. Some games players excel at one type of game or the other. A few very good players excel at both game types.

I cover the three basic skills required to play backgammon in the next three sections.

Making use of arithmetic

How you move your checkers is governed by the numbers that come up when you roll the dice. As in any game involving dice, arithmetic and understanding numbers are pretty significant in playing backgammon.

As in all great games, you can apply skills at different levels and if you're a wizard at arithmetic, you may be able to do things that some of your opponents can't.

If you haven't got a mathematical mind, don't worry in the slightest. I have many friends who don't concern themselves about the arithmetic at all and still get hours of enjoyment from playing backgammon. I give you the basics and then you can decide how much effort you want to put into this aspect of the game.

Practising pattern recognition

In your daily life, you do certain things again and again. After you've done something once or twice, you remember how to do it the next time without thinking; this is *pattern recognition*. You can apply the same principle to backgammon.

Comprehending the vast number of possible backgammon positions is almost impossible. If you had to analyse each position from scratch every time you played the game, it wouldn't be much fun. Luckily, positions and types of positions constantly recur, so if you can remember the strategy you used last time you had a similar position, then you can make use of that knowledge to accelerate your decision-making process in your current situation.

Over time you build up a mental library of positions and make increasing use of that library every time you play. The very best players have a huge library and the ability to recall information from it.

Don't worry if this process sounds quite daunting. You can quickly build up your own mental library and start to use it almost immediately. This book provides you with the first entries!

Being mindful of psychology

Backgammon has swings of fortune unlike nearly any other game. You must be able to cope with the adrenalin surge that takes place when you go from zero to hero in the time it takes to roll the dice. The reverse is also true – you have to be able to cope with losing from the most unlikely positions. More importantly, you have to understand and make use of the impact of such swings of fortune on your opponent.

Understanding your opponent's mental make-up can be very useful in backgammon; in this book I show you how to apply pressure on your opponent to your advantage.

Never forget that you're playing another human being. Unlike computers, human beings make mistakes, sometimes technical in nature, sometimes emotional. A calm temperament is a huge asset when playing backgammon!

Combining Three Parts into a Whole Game

Players divide the game of backgammon into three phases – opening, middle game, and end game. You need to understand each part in its own right but also how the three combine to make the whole. Playing backgammon is a little like listening to a symphony – you enjoy the whole thing but you also understand the contribution that each movement makes to the overall effect.

Here's a quick breakdown of what each phase entails:

- ✔ **The opening:** The main objective of the opening move is to activate your forces (checkers). Unlike chess, you rarely find comprehensive analyses of opening backgammon moves and subsequent responses but I cover this crucial area of the game in detail in Chapter 4.

- ✔ **The middle game:** The middle game is the most complex area of the game where the two armies seek to gain the upper hand and skirmishes and full-bloodied battles are the order of the day.

  To help you understand the middle game, I break it down into different types and then create broad principles for each type. Chapters 7 and 8 address the middle game.

- ✔ **The end game:** Finally the armies (largely) disengage and each player seeks to bear off his checkers as quickly as possible and win the game. This phase may seem simple, but often contact between the opposing forces late into the game adds to the complexity of the end game. I cover the end game in Chapters 9 to 11.

Choosing among the Different Ways to Play the Game

You can play backgammon purely for fun and without the doubling cube. This style of play is common in the Middle East. But more often, playing backgammon involves using the doubling cube and playing for some sort of stake. I talk about the various styles in the next sections.

A single game of backgammon can take anywhere from 30 seconds to 30 minutes, so often players define a session by number of games (best of three, for example) or period of time (games won in an hour, for instance). I like to play for three to four hours at a time. (My personal record is 27 hours!)

Wagering one-on-one

Normally you play head-to-head backgammon for a stake, however nominal, which adds a level of interest to the game. The two main styles when money is involved are:

- **Money play:** Each game is treated separately and played for an agreed stake. At the end of each game, the loser pays the winner the agreed initial stake multiplied by the value of the doubling cube and further multiplied by 2 for a gammon or 3 for a backgammon (I explain these terms in Chapter 2).

- **Match play:** The players agree that the winner is the first to reach an agreed number of points. So, a seven-point match is one in which the first player to score seven points wins the match.

  Match play is more complex than money play because you have to factor the score into your decisions as to how to move the checkers and, more importantly, how to handle the doubling cube.

Entering the chouette

The final and most exciting way to play the game is known as *chouette* (shoo-et), which I explain in detail in Chapter 12. In this form of the game, one player plays against two or more other players who are allowed to consult with one another over their moves. The single player and the numerous opponents together form a chouette.

Playing chouettes is a great way to pick up the game quickly. If you listen to a group of good players discuss a difficult position, you can discover more in five minutes than you'd get from five hours of play against a weak opponent.

I've spent countless hours of my life playing chouettes and enjoy this form of the game most. Three (or four or five) heads are generally reckoned to be better than one but I have proof that this assumption is not always the case!

The origins of backgammon

Backgammon is one of the oldest games in existence. Its history can be traced back nearly 5,000 years to its origins in Mesopotamia (modern-day Iraq). The world's oldest set of dice (made from human bone) were recently discovered in that part of the world.

Backgammon first became popular under the Romans, who called it *Duodecum Scripta et Tabulae* or 'Tables' for short. Emperor Claudius had a board built on his chariot.

The word *backgammon* first appeared in writing in 1645, although nobody knows for sure where the name originated. The game itself appears frequently in art and literature, perhaps most famously in Hieronymus Bosch's painting *The Garden of Earthly Delights* and Shakespeare's play *Love's Labour's Lost.*

Although popular during Victorian England, by the 1920s backgammon was losing its appeal. Luckily two things happened more or less in parallel: the concept of doubling was introduced and the variation of play known as the chouette arrived. From these developments, backgammon has never looked back and indeed with the advent of online play is again growing in popularity. Unlike chess, significant advances in backgammon theory have happened only in the last 20 years and can be traced directly to the arrival of powerful computers using neural net technology.

Neural net technology enables computers to play at the same level as the best players in the world. Because of their processing power computers are able to perform analysis impossible for humans. This processing power has enabled humans to test theories that were impossible to test 20 years ago and as a result today's expert is light years removed from his 1970s counterpart.

In time, no doubt, computers will be the strongest players in the world!

Chapter 2

Playing the Game

· ·

In This Chapter

▶ Tumbling the numbers

▶ Going point-to-point

▶ Celebrating a win

· ·

*I*n this chapter, I look at actually rolling the dice and moving the checkers. I describe how you move the checkers around the board and the perils they face on that journey. Finally I describe how you take the checkers off the board and actually win the game!

Rolling the Dice

Each player has two dice, quite often the same colour as her checkers, though not always. Each player also has a dice shaker.

When you take your turn to play, you shake the dice vigorously in the shaker and then roll the dice into the right-hand side of the board as you face it – even if you're left-handed. Every game has its odd procedures and customs, and rolling into the right-hand board is one of backgammon's.

For a roll to be legal, both dice must land flat on the right-hand side of the board. You must re-roll *both* dice if:

    ✔ Either die misses the right-hand board and lands on the table or on the left-hand board.

    ✔ The dice are *cocked.* Both of the following situations result in *cocked dice*:

        • Either die lands on one of the checkers or at an angle.

        • Only one die leaves the dice shaker.

When you finish moving your checkers, you complete your turn by picking up your dice and putting them back in your shaker. Until you lift your dice from the board, it's still your turn and you can re-do any or all of your moves. Once you return your dice to the shaker, your opponent takes his turn.

Current backgammon rules say that if you roll your dice before your opponent has picked up his dice then he may make his move based on the foreknowledge of what your roll is going to be. This foreknowledge is a huge advantage to give away, so always make sure that your opponent has completed his move before you roll your dice.

Agreeing on the Notation

Before I explain how to move the checkers as dictated by the dice, we need to agree on some form of notation, and because I'm the one writing, you, dear reader, get to agree with me.

Some of what I say now may not be immediately clear to you because I haven't yet discussed the types of move in detail, so please consider the following as a reference section and come back to it as necessary.

Backgammon survived for years without a generally agreed way of recording moves – perhaps because nobody recorded games before the 1970s (unbelievable but true!). Sometime in that decade, the backgammon world came to its senses and a standard format was agreed. I explain those agreements in the next sections.

Indicating the roll of the dice

Dice rolls are given as two numbers. The higher number is shown first. A roll of a 3 and a 1 is shown as 31. Doubles are shown as a pair. Double 5 would be 55.

Numbering the points on the board

So that two people (in this case, you and I) can understand each other when talking about locations on a backgammon board, the backgammon powers that be (or powers that were in the 1970s) devised a system for numbering the 24 points on a backgammon board. Simply put, you assign the number 1 to the first point in your home board and go around the board until you number all 24 points.

Figure 2-1 shows a set-up board with the points numbered for both Black and White. Each point actually has two numbers, one for each player's perspective. When Black is on roll, she calls the fourth point in her home board her 4-point. That same point becomes the 21-point when White takes his next turn to play.

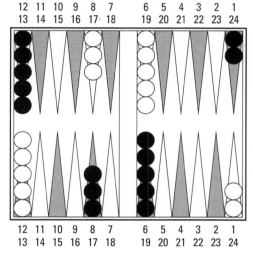

12 11 10 9 8 7   6 5 4 3 2 1
13 14 15 16 17 18   19 20 21 22 23 24

12 11 10 9 8 7   6 5 4 3 2 1
13 14 15 16 17 18   19 20 21 22 23 24

Figure 2-1: A starting board with points numbered for both players.

Figures are normally numbered from the point of view of the player whose home board is at the bottom of the diagram – in Figure 2-1, that's Black.

Showing how the checkers move

Each move of a checker is shown by giving its start point and end point separated by a forward slash (/). The point numbers are based on the point of view of the player on roll. So, 8/5 means that a checker moves from the 8-point to the 5-point, for example.

If the roll is *doubles* (both dice show the same number) and two or more checkers move from the same start point to the same end point, the number of checkers moved is enclosed in brackets after the moves. So, 8/4(2) indicates that two checkers moved from the 8-point to the 4-point.

When you record a whole game, each move is numbered.

Sometimes a checker is hit from the board and has to re-enter from the bar. In this case, the start point is shown as 'bar'. If a player is on the bar and fails to re-enter, this is shown by '0' or the word 'fan'.

Occasionally, a player can't make any legal play. In this instance, the dice roll is followed by the words 'no play'.

If a move includes hitting one of your opponent's checkers, an asterisk (*) is added at the end. For example, if you move a checker from your 13-point to your 8-point and in doing so hit an opponent's checker, the notation is 13/8*. (I talk about hitting an opponent in 'Hitting and re-entering' a little later in the chapter.)

At the end of the game when you bear off a checker, you record the point number and the word *off*, so taking a checker off your 5-point is shown as 5/off.

Last but not least, you have to record the action of the doubling cube, that strange die with big numbers on it. At the start of the game, the doubling cube sits on the side of the board showing the number 64 (the doubling cube has no 1 so 64 represents 1), which is the cube's starting position. As the cube comes into play, it sits near the home board of the player who currently owns it and displays its current value. If either player doubles, the move is shown as 'double'. The opponent's response is recorded as 'take' or 'drop'.

This information may not make sense immediately. As you begin to play, though, it will slot into place.

Moving the Checkers

You're now ready to move your checkers and the following sections tell you how to do just that.

Starting the game

To start the game, each player rolls one die. The player with the higher number makes the first move using the numbers from her own die and that of her opponent. If both players roll the same number, they re-roll until one player has a higher number.

If both players roll the same number, by mutual agreement they can double the nominal stake, which is known as an *automatic double*. Back in the 1970s, when oil money fuelled high stake games, the habit was to play unlimited automatics, so that if both players rolled the same number six times, the stake would be 64 times the original stake! Unlimited automatics are like wounded tigers – animals to be avoided at all costs!

Making moves

You move your checkers in accordance with the numbers shown on the dice, treating each number as a separate move. For example, if the two dice show a 4 and a 2, you can move one checker four points (known as *pips*) and a different checker two points or you may move one checker six points. The bar doesn't count as a point.

When you roll a *double* – the number on both dice is the same – you're entitled to four moves rather than just two. For example, if you roll two fives, you move four fives. Rolling a double is normally an advantage.

You must play both numbers of your roll if you're legally able to do so (and four numbers if possible when you roll a double). If you can't play your entire roll, follow these rules:

- ✔ If you can play only one of your two numbers, you must play the one you're able to.
- ✔ If you can move either but only one of the two numbers, you must play the higher.
- ✔ If you roll a double, you must play as many of the four numbers as you can.

If you can't play at all, you forfeit your turn.

Landing on open points

The final destination for your checker, as well as the interim point if you're moving one checker both numbers, must be an *open point*, which is a point not already occupied by two or more of your opponent's checkers.

You can pile up any number of your own checkers on a single point, but if your opponent has two or more checkers on a point, your checker can't stop there or even use it as an intermediate point when using both dice to move a single checker.

If you roll 42 and want to move one checker six spaces, the point two or four spaces from the starting point must be open.

Hitting a blot

A single checker on a point is called a *blot*, and an opponent's blot is often a good place to land on. When you land on a point occupied by just one of your opponent's checkers, you knock that checker off that point and off the board.

Landing on one of your opponent's solitary checkers is called a *hit*. The hit checker is removed from the board and placed on the bar. It must re-enter the playing field into your home board. The upcoming 'Hitting and re-entering' section explains this procedure in detail.

Getting practical with an example

Let me present a practical example of moving the checkers.

In Figure 2-2, Black has a 6 and a 1 to play, as shown by the two black dice in the middle of Black's home board.

Black's options for using the 6 are: 24/18, 13/7, or 8/2. If she moves 24/18, she can't move that same checker 18/17 with the 1 because White owns the 17-point because he has three checkers on it. Similarly if Black moves 8/2, she cannot then move 2/1 because White owns her 1-point.

With the 1, Black can move 24/23, 8/7, or 6/5 but not 13/12 because White owns Black's 12-point.

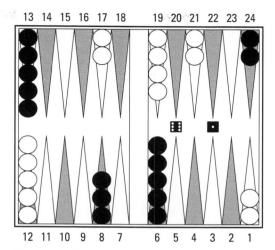

Figure 2-2: Playing a 61.

The best choice for this roll is to move 13/7 with the 6 and 8/7 with the 1, as shown in Figure 2-3. Black improves her position because she now owns a new point, her 7-point, or as this point is more commonly known, her *bar-point*.

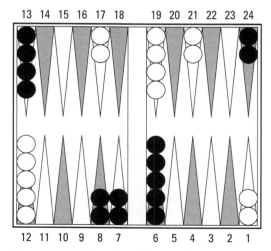

Figure 2-3: Having played 61 correctly.

Figure 2-4 shows another example.

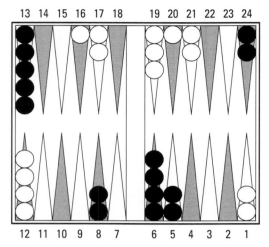

Figure 2-4: Legal moves.

If Black rolls any 4 she can hit the blot on White's 4-point. She can also hit it with 31 played 24/23/20* but note that 24/21/20* is illegal because White owns the 21-point.

Notice also that if Black rolls 53, she'd like to hit the blot on the 16-point but neither 24/21/16* or 24/19/16* is legal because White owns both the 19 and 21 points. If Black does roll 53, she can play 8/3, 6/3 taking ownership of her own 3-point.

In general, taking ownership of a new point is a good idea, and making points next to each other is even better because the more points you have in a row, the more difficult your opponent finds it to leap over them. The ultimate block is a *prime* of six points in a row. Trapping an opponent's checker behind your prime gives you a huge advantage because your opponent can't get past your prime as the biggest number on the die is 6 and you own six points in a row. He can't leave until you move your checkers off at least one point.

Hitting and re-entering

Hitting an opponent's blot – a single checker on a point – and having your own blots hit by your opponent brings a lot of excitement, and sometimes anguish, to the game. In this section, I explain the mechanics of hitting a blot and its aftermath.

When one of your checkers is hit by your opponent, he removes the checker from its point and places it on the bar between the home and outer boards (see Chapter 1 for information on the boards).

On your next turn, you must re-enter the checker into your opponent's home board before you can make any other move. Where you re-enter is determined by the dice.

To re-enter you need to roll a number on at least one of the dice that equates to an open point in your opponent's board. Remember that an open point is one that has less than two of your opponent's checkers on it.

Figure 2-5 shows that Black has been hit and her hit checker is now on the bar. To re-enter, she must roll a 1, 2, 3, or 4. Note that 5s and 6s are no good because White owns those points. That means that if Black rolls 55, 66, or 56, she must forfeit her turn. Unlike real life, staying on the bar isn't fun!

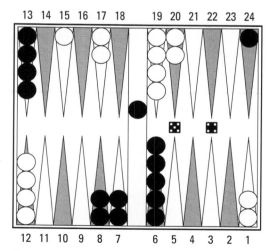

Figure 2-5: Entering from the bar.

If Black rolls 54, she must re-enter on White's 4-point by playing bar/21 and then playing her 5. Her more sensible options are 13/8 or 21/16.

You may have two or more checkers on the bar – I hope not too frequently. In that case, you must re-enter all your checkers before you can make any other move. You may have worked out that having lots of checkers on the bar isn't a winning game plan!

You cannot have more than 15 checkers, of either or both colours, on the bar at the same time.

If all six points on the opponent's home board are closed and you have one or more checkers on the bar, you forfeit your turn until a point in the home board becomes open again.

Bearing off

To end a game, you take all your checkers off the board. If you're the first player to accomplish this action, you win. (The next section covers winning in all its glory.)

Your first objective in a game is to get all 15 of your checkers into your home board. After you do that – and only after you get all your checkers in – you can start to take them off the board, a process called *bearing off*. Once borne off, a checker never returns.

If one of your checkers is hit and sent to the bar while you're bearing off, you have to stop bearing off until the errant checker reaches your home board again. Having even one checker outside your home board prevents you from bearing off.

Often both players get all their checkers into their home boards at nearly the same time and then the game becomes simply a dice-rolling contest to see who can get their checkers off first.

Paying attention to the points

As with every other move in backgammon, bearing off is governed by the roll of the dice. Your home board has six points, numbered 1 to 6, and each point corresponds to a number on the dice. (The Cheat Sheet at the front of the book shows the numbered points, which are 1 to 6 left-to-right if your home board is on your left and 1 to 6 starting at the far right if your home board is on your right.) You roll the dice and bear off checkers sitting on the corresponding points. When you roll doubles, you bear off four checkers from the appropriate point.

Rolling 54 lets you bear off a checker from your 5-point and one from your 4-point.

If you don't have any checkers on a point corresponding to the number you've rolled but you do have checkers on higher numbered points, you must move from one of the higher points. For example, if you roll a 5 and have no checkers on your 5-point but you do have checkers on your 6-point, you must play 6/1 with the 5.

If you roll a number bigger than any of your occupied points, you bear off checkers from your highest occupied point.

You roll 65 but only have checkers on your 1-point, 2-point, and 3-point. You bear off two checkers from your 3-point. If you have just one checker on your 3-point, you bear off that checker and one checker from your 2-point.

Bearing off with an enemy in your camp — or in your home board

Sometimes while you're bearing off your checkers, your opponent still has some of his checkers in your home board or on the bar. Such cases require conservative tactics to ensure that you don't get a blot hit and that caution becomes your watchword. The last thing you want is to have a checker hit, sent to the bar, and have to come all the way around the board again.

One of the often forgotten (or maybe just infrequently remembered) rules of backgammon is that you can make your moves in any order. Black's situation in Figure 2-6 shows the benefits of making use of this tactic.

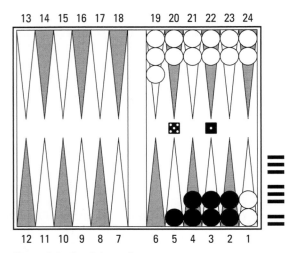

Figure 2-6: A subtle tactic.

Black has already taken off eight checkers (indicated by the discs on the right-hand-side of the figure) and now rolls 51. If White's two checkers weren't still in Black's home board, Black could play 5/off, then 4/3, 3/2, or 2/1. It may look as if she has to move 5/off and 4/3 anyway, which leaves a blot on her 4-point. So if White were to roll a 3 next turn and hit the blot, he would be right back in the game with Black stuck on the bar because White's home board is closed to her.

However, Black can choose to move the 1 first, playing 5/4 and then using the 5 to remove a checker from the 4-point, which is the highest occupied point. That way she doesn't leave any blots.

Winning the Game

Backgammon at its simplest is a racing game, but if it were only that it wouldn't have lasted 5,000 years. As the preceding sections make clear, the hitting and recirculating of checkers adds a level of complexity, even before I introduce the most complicated element of all – the doubling cube, which I explain in Chapter 6.

The first player to take off all his or her checkers is the winner, but three different classes of winning exist:

- ✔ **Single game:** One player takes off all her checkers before her opponent bears off all of his, although the opponent has taken off at least one of his checkers.

  This type of win is worth one unit of whatever stake you're playing for. If you stake £5 per point, for example, the winning player banks £5.

- ✔ **Gammon:** A player bears off all her checkers before her opponent has borne off any of his. A gammon occurs about once in every five games.

  A gammon pays double the nominal stake, so a stake of £5 gets you £10.

- ✔ **Backgammon:** The pinnacle of the game! A backgammon is won when a player bears off all her checkers before her opponent has borne off any of his *and* the opponent has a checker (or checkers) still on the bar or in the winner's home board. A backgammon occurs approximately once every hundred games.

  A backgammon triples the stake.

Chapter 3

Looking at Basic Backgammon Tactics

*I*n this chapter, I cover the basic arithmetic created by using two dice, the simple tactics of the game, and how to start thinking about which moves you should play and why. I take you beyond a basic understanding of the rules to selecting moves based on at least a rudimentary game plan.

Understanding Dice and Numbers

Each player has two dice and rolls both of them together except in the first roll of a game. Understanding the possible outcomes of these rolls is a key component of backgammon strategy. In the following sections, I explain the possibilities and how to put these possibilities to work for you.

Reading a dice table

Rolling two dice together produces 36 possible outcomes, as shown in Table 3-1. The outcome for one die is shown in normal script and the other in *italics*.

Table 3-1		Outcomes of Rolling Two Dice			
Dice	*1*	*2*	*3*	*4*	*5*	*6*
1	1*1*	12	1*3*	14	15	1*6*
2	2*1*	22	23	24	25	26
3	3*1*	32	3*3*	34	35	36
4	4*1*	42	4*3*	44	45	46
5	5*1*	52	5*3*	54	55	5*6*
6	6*1*	62	6*3*	64	65	6*6*

Each individual number shows up 11 times in the dice table, and the chances of rolling a specific number are 11 in 36. The odds that a roll contains one of two specific numbers are 20 in 36. To prove this calculation, count the number of times each number appears in the dice table in Table 3-1, then choose two numbers, say 5 and 6, and count how many times one or the other appears. Each of the six doubles occurs only once in the 36 outcomes and each of the non-doubles twice. For example, you can roll a 21 as 2*1* or 1*2*. Thus you're twice as likely to roll a 21 as you are to roll a 22.

In backgammon, you often need to know how many ways you can roll a specific number. How many rolls contain a 6, for example? Scanning for 6s in the dice table, you see that the answer is 11. But you can also get to 6 by rolling 5*1*, 1*5*, 4*2*, 2*4*, 3*3*, and 2*2* (double 3 actually gives you a total of 12 and double 2 gives 8, but 6 is an increment in both). So if you need to roll a 6 to hit an opponent's blot (Chapter 2 explains what a blot is) and the opponent doesn't hold any points in between that blot and your checker, then you've 17 ways to roll a 6 – nearly 50 per cent of all 36 possible rolls! Contrast that figure with the number of ways to roll a 1 – only 11.

Knowing how many ways you can roll any specific number naturally (the roll contains the desired number) or in combination is very useful. Table 3-2 shows the chances that a roll contains or combines to the numbers from 1 to 24.

Table 3-2	Number-rolling Odds
Number	Chance of Rolling It
1	11
2	12
3	14
4	15
5	15
6	17
7	6
8	6
9	5
10	3
11	2
12	3
15	1
16	1
18	1
20	1
24	1

Using the dice table

How do you make use of the information in the dice table? Well, let me offer some examples.

In Figure 3-1, Black has to get his last two checkers into his home board before he can start bearing off. He rolls 63, which forces him to play 10/4 (you *must* move if you can and the only way Black can use the 6 is to move 10/4). Black must now decide how to play the 3. The single checker on the 10-point is a blot no matter what he does, but should he play 10/7 with that checker or move 6/3 or 4/1?

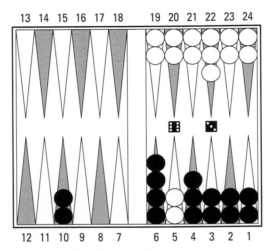

Figure 3-1: Black leaves a blot.

The answer lies in the dice table (refer to Table 3-1 in the previous section). If Black plays 10/7, he leaves White only 11 chances of hitting the blot because White can hit him with all the 2s except 11, which is blocked because Black owns his own 6-point. If Black plays 6/3 or 4/1, White has 15 hitting numbers (any direct 5 or any combination of 5). It makes sense to leave as few hitting numbers as possible, so 10/7 is the correct play.

From this example, you can create a general rule: When you have to leave a blot within six points of your opponent's checker, leave the blot as close to the enemy as possible.

In the second example, in Figure 3-2, Black has to play 51. If he moves 8/3 or 6/1 with the 5, he leaves White a *direct shot*, a chance to hit a blot with a single number from one of the two dice. An *indirect shot* requires the total of both dice to hit the blot.

TIP

If you've the choice between leaving your opponent a direct shot or an indirect shot, leaving an indirect shot improves your chances of not getting hit.

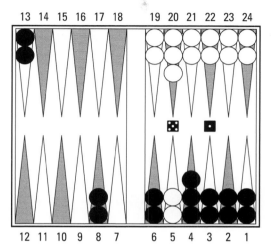

Figure 3-2: Choosing between direct and indirect shots.

Black sensibly plays 13/8 with the 5. He can play the 1 by moving 13/12 or 4/3. (He doesn't move 8/7 with the 1 because that exposes two blots.)

Black needs to consider whether a difference exists between leaving the blot on the 13-point or moving it to the 12-point. On the 13-point, the blot is eight points away from White's checkers and therefore White has six hitting numbers. On the 12-point, the blot is seven points away and also subject to six hitting numbers. A dead heat! Backgammon rarely produces a dead heat as is the case here. Now Black can look at his options if the blot isn't hit and determines that, as he'll find it easier to bring the blot to safety in his home board from his 12-point as one 6 can do the trick, he plays 13/12.

You can also use the dice table to calculate your chances of re-entering from the bar, as White faces in Figure 3-3.

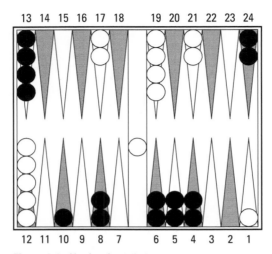

Figure 3-3: Hoping for 1, 2, 3.

White has a checker on the bar and must roll a 1, 2, or 3 to re-enter the board. From the dice table, you can quickly see that 27 rolls contain a 1, 2, or 3. As 27 is 75 per cent of the 36 possible outcomes, White therefore can enter 75 per cent of the time. The remaining 25 per cent of the time, she languishes on the bar.

Please don't be intimidated by the numbers – you'll soon be quoting these percentages as second nature and wondering what all the fuss was about.

Even though Black owns 50 per cent of his home board points, White enters 75 per cent of the time – that's just the way the arithmetic happens to pan out! If Black owned five of his home board points, White would still enter 11 times out of 36, or roughly 30 per cent of the time.

Starting Out with the Fundamentals

In these sections, I fill you in on what constitutes a good move and what makes a bad move in backgammon and try to clearly spell out the basic ideas of the game.

Making points

Making a new point by moving two or more of your checkers to the same open point is a good idea. As in war, gaining new territory is normally a good tactic. In backgammon, owning points gives you two key advantages:

- ✔ They provide you with safe places for your checkers to land as they travel round the board.
- ✔ They make it more difficult for your opponent to move his checkers around the board.

Making points that are next to each other is also a good idea because doing so makes it more difficult for your opponent to get her checkers past yours. Figure 3-4 shows the board after Black opened the game with a roll of 31 and played 8/5, 6/5, making his own 5-point.

You can use any opening roll where the numbers on the dice differ by two to make a new point in your home board. A 42 roll lets you make your 4-point by moving 8/4, 6/4, a 53 makes your 3-point, and a 64 makes your 2-point.

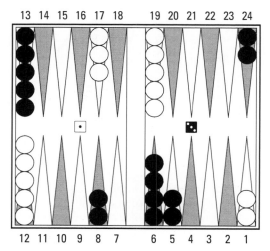

Figure 3-4: Making a point.

This simple move is a significant improvement for Black. Now White can't play 4s and 5s with her two rearmost checkers and Black has the start of a nice block. He owns his 5-point, 6-point, and 8-point. If he can put two checkers on his 7-point, he'll have four points in a row.

A specific advantage gained from making points in your home board is that doing so reduces your opponent's chances of entering from the bar, if you hit any of your opponent's checkers.

Making points at home

Sometimes you have a choice of which point to make, as Black does in Figure 3-5.

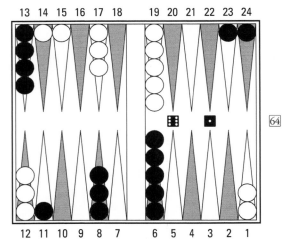

Figure 3-5: Choosing which point to make.

Black has two reasonable choices with his 61 roll. He can play 11/5, 6/5, making his 5-point, or he can play 13/7, 8/7, making his bar-point. At first sight, not much difference exists between the two moves, but a couple of factors come into play:

- ✔ A point in your home board is normally better than one in the outer boards.

- ✔ Checkers on the 6-point are the most difficult ones to get into play, so using one efficiently with the 11/5, 6/5 move is a good idea.

Naming the points

Over the years various names have been given to key points on the board:

- Backgammon legend Paul Magriel named the 5-point the 'golden point' back in the 1970s and the name stuck. He correctly identified that the two 5-points are the two most important points on the board.

- Another bit of backgammon terminology – the 1-point is commonly referred to as the 'ace-point'.

- The 7-point is much more commonly referred to as the 'bar-point' – maybe because this point is so close to the bar? That's my guess, anyway.

Making points in your opponent's home

Quite often, your choice is between making a point in your opponent's home board or your own home board. Check out Black's position in Figure 3-6.

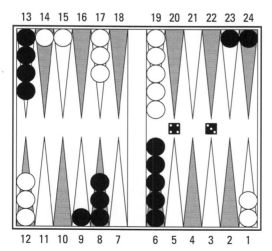

Figure 3-6: Making a point at home or abroad.

Black can use his roll of 43 to make his own 5-point with 9/5, 8/5, or his opponent's 5-point (his own 20-point) with 24/20, 23/20.

Normally, making a point in your opponent's home board is smart, if you can. Any point in your opponent's home board is known as an *anchor*, and the more advanced the anchor – the closer this point is to your home board – the better off you are.

Another rule of thumb is to make the point that's more difficult to make. Notice that in Figure 3-6, if Black goes ahead and makes his own 5-point with 9/5, 8/5, White has lots of ways to make her own 5-point next turn. Therefore Black needs to make sure that he grabs that point now and hope he can make his own 5-point later on.

Building primes

Making points is good, but making primes is even better! Having a *prime* means owning two or more points next to each other. The ultimate is a six-point prime with some of your opponent's checkers trapped behind it. Her checkers can leave only when you give them permission to do so by opening a point!

A 61 roll builds a new point on your bar-point (13/7, 8/7) and creates a three-point prime that can help to block your opponent's backmost checkers.

Figure 3-7 shows Black with a perfect prime. White also has six points in a row in her home board, and at first sight the two positions look similar. But then you notice that White's two back checkers are still stuck on Black's 1-point! Black has a six-point prime, called a *full prime* or a *perfect prime* extending from his bar-point to his 2-point, effectively locking in White's two checkers. A prime is still perfect even if no enemy checkers are trapped behind it.

However, nothing lasts forever and on his next turn Black probably needs to move those two checkers from his bar-point into his home board so that he can start bearing off. White can then escape and move her back men.

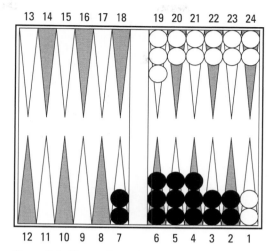

Figure 3-7: The perfect prime.

Black has a winning position as he can probably bear his checkers off long before White can get her two back checkers out, move them around the board, and bear off all her checkers. But, although you may think that White is completely lost here, in Chapter 10 I show how she can win despite having an apparently losing position. Although full primes are the ideal, four- and five-point primes are not to be sniffed at and can quite often be good enough to win games.

Building primes is one strategy in which 5-points are very important. If you can make your own 5-point, then you only need to make your bar-point to have a four-point prime from your 5-point to your 8-point. Equally, owning your opponent's 5-point makes it difficult for her to prime your back checkers.

Hitting your opponent's checkers

As a general rule, hitting your opponent's checkers is a good idea. A hit checker must go on the bar and then start its journey home all over again. As backgammon is a racing game, it makes sense to set your opponent back in the race whenever you can.

Hitting one man

Figure 3-8 shows a trivial example of a good hit. White had to leave a blot on her 11-point. Black now rolls 22 and chortles with glee (quietly to himself, of course, because he's a gentleman). He hits the blot with 20/18/16/14* and uses his last 2 to move 20/18.

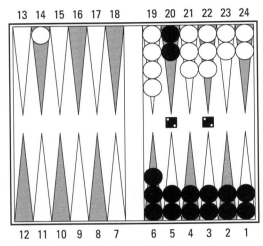

Figure 3-8: A winning hit.

From being in a position in which he has to get two checkers around the board, while White has just one to get into her home board before she can start bearing off, Black is now nearly certain to win the game. He has a perfect home board and White won't be able to enter from the bar for some time. By the time Black opens up a point to enable White to get in, Black can have many of his checkers safely borne off and be well ahead in the race.

Making a point or making a hit

You often have to choose among several good things to do with your roll. Sometimes, your choice is between hitting and making a new point. Figure 3-9 shows an example from the second move of a game.

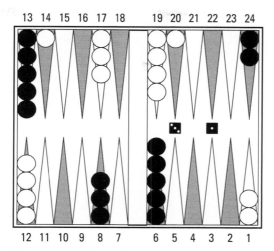

Figure 3-9: Making a choice.

Black can do two good things with his roll of 31. He can make his own 5-point with 8/5, 6/5 or he can hit the blot on White's 5-point with 24/20*. In this situation, hitting is better for a number of reasons:

- ✔ Hitting sets White back in the race because a checker that started in White's home board now has to travel all the way around the board to get back to where it started.

- ✔ Placing a checker on White's 5-point and thereby *starting a point* puts Black in position to own his opponent's 5-point if he rolls a 4 on his next turn.

- ✔ Passing up the opportunity to hit White's blot and making his own 5-point instead gives White the quite likely chance to make her own 5-point on her next roll, and thus equalise the positions.

Hitting can be wrong

Figure 3-10 shows a situation in which hitting is the wrong move. In this position, Black could use his 31 roll to move 24/20* and hit White's blot. But Black can do much better by playing 8/5, 6/5 and building a five-point prime. That long-term asset gives him a huge advantage.

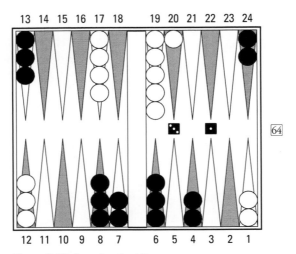

Figure 3-10: Ignoring the hit.

Much of backgammon is about choosing between different plans and plays and this illustration is a classic example. This problem combines two themes – hitting and priming.

Hitting two checkers

If hitting one checker is good, then hitting two checkers must be even better. Consider Black's position in Figure 3-11.

Black has four 4s to play. He plays the first two 24/20*/16*, putting the two White blots on the bar, and then plays 8/4(2) with the remaining two 4s. Making a new point in the home board is much stronger than 24/20*/16*(2) because it helps to prevent White from re-entering from the bar.

This roll gives Black huge advantages:

- Black puts two of White's checkers on the bar.
- Black gains in the race because he's rolled 16 pips himself and sent two white checkers to the bar.
- Black makes a new point in his home board.

All these advantages with one roll of the dice!

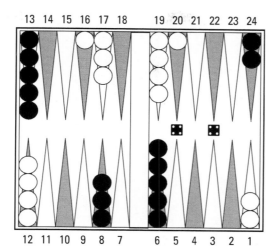

Figure 3-11: Hitting twice.

Having two checkers on the bar is a major disadvantage because, unless you roll a double, you spend your entire next turn just entering your checkers back onto the board. Quite often – depending upon the strength of your opponent's home board – you may be left with at least one checker on the bar after your turn.

In the example in Figure 3-11, if White's next roll is 64, both her checkers must stay on the bar because they've no legal entry points (Black owns both his 4-point and his 6-point).

Beware of leaving too many blots; they can all end up together on the bar!

Hitting to gain tempo

Not all hits are obvious, particularly when you're learning the game. Figure 3-12 shows an example from early in the game. White started the game by playing her roll of 43 by moving 24/20, 13/10. Black now has to play a 21. A beginner may look at moves such as 24/23, 24/22, or 24/21, but in fact the best move is 13/11, 6/5*.

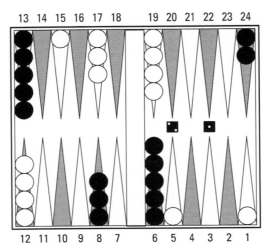

Figure 3-12: Hitting off the 5-point.

The reasons why this move is the right one certainly aren't obvious, so let me explain:

  ✔ White made a bold play to start a point and build an anchor on Black's 5-point. Black certainly isn't going to let her have it without a fight!

  ✔ Black deprives White of half her next roll because she has to use it to re-enter from the bar. This action is called *gaining a tempo.*

The odds of getting hit back are quite high but that isn't so important in the opening where re-entering on your opponent's board is easy. The trick is to fight for key points in the opening and not let your opponent have an easy time.

Left unmolested, White can do all manner of good things next turn. By hitting her, Black vastly reduces White's potential for her next turn and seizes the tempo for himself.

Choosing Your Move

How on earth do you always make the best play? The simple answer is that you don't – no one does. If everyone always played perfectly, the game would've been abandoned years ago and the world would have moved on to something else. Not even the best players make the best move all the time; the game is just too complex.

In any backgammon position, you nearly always have a best move. The move may not be best by much, maybe only a fraction of a per cent in winning chances, but it still has an edge over its rivals. Occasionally two moves are the same but that's rare indeed.

In the following sections, I concentrate on making sure that you at least try to see the possible plays.

Identifying candidate plays

The first step in seeing possible moves, called *candidate plays*, is to get comfortable with the starting position of your checkers and what you can do with certain rolls of the dice.

No matter what positions your checkers are in, you usually have lots of legal ways to play your roll. Your job is to see which moves make sense and then choose between them. In the early days, you make mistakes but that happens with any game; just accept them and move on.

You need to look for plays that improve your position in some way, for example, by making a new point or escaping a back checker, and then choose between them.

One of the great advantages of the rules of backgammon is that you can try out as many moves as you like, so long as you don't pick up your dice. Particularly when you're learning, I advise you to try out moves, just don't take so long that your opponent becomes irritated!

Black has many possible plays for his 53 roll in Figure 3-13. But just a little playing experience leads you to appreciate that the only two real candidate plays are 24/16* (broken down into 24/21, 21/16*) and 8/3, 6/3. Both moves do something good: the first one hits an opponent's checker and sends it to the bar; the second move makes a new home-board point.

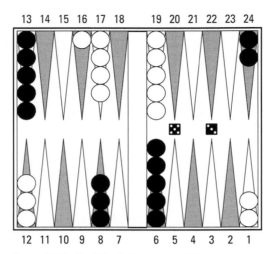

Figure 3-13: Deciding between candidates.

Actually 24/16* does two good things: it sends White's checker to the bar, and it gets one of Black's two rearmost checkers on its journey home. A move that does two good things is likely to be the winner and so such is the case here.

You can't make a move if you don't see it! Many errors are made by a player deliberating long and hard between Play A and Play B, when he hasn't even considered the best play – Play C. Make sure that you don't miss a candidate play!

Everyone misses plays. To limit your misses, ensure that you take long enough to study the position and identify the candidates. As you become familiar with the game, you'll miss plays far less often but you'll still miss them occasionally. I'm still missing plays after 30 years' practice!

Selecting the best play

After you identify your candidate plays, you must choose what you believe to be the best play, which isn't always easy, believe me.

Missing a play is criminal but misjudging a play is acceptable because nobody makes the best play every single time.

Ultimately your decision on each play is based on your own skills and knowledge. Good judgement comes with time and experience. As you play more your pattern recognition improves, as does your knowledge of the strategies and tactics of the game. You also realise that psychology can play a part in your decision making. With practice, you'll make the right decision the majority of the time and your mistakes will be small ones.

If you persevere, you can make the right move in positions such as the one facing Black in Figure 3-14.

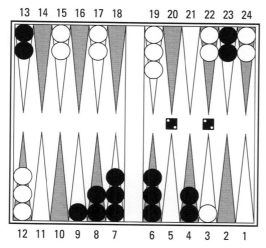

Figure 3-14: Making the right move.

Small doubles are often difficult to play correctly because they present so many different options. One of the best players in the world, Nack Ballard, took over five minutes to determine all the candidate plays for this double 2 (at least six reasonable plays are possible), analyse them, and then make his move.

The move he chose is 13/11, 13/9, 7/5. This play threatens to build a full prime in front of White's rearmost checker next turn and exposes the blot on Black's 5-point with only a direct hit by a 2.

Move selection is one of the most difficult things in backgammon; please be patient with yourself!

Chapter 4

Making the Opening Move

In This Chapter

▶ Planning what to do with your opening move

▶ Running through the best and 'okay, I'll take it' opening rolls

▶ Responding to the first move

*T*his chapter looks at how to play the opening roll. As in many other games, the first couple of moves can often define the whole course of a game.

You may think that in a game that is 5,000 years old the experts would agree on how to play the opening roll. Surprisingly they don't, quite, and considerable debate still occurs on how to play 10 of the 15 possible opening rolls.

Understanding Opening Objectives

The opening phase of a backgammon game can be anything from a couple of moves to nine, ten, or even more. Both sides jockey for position and seek to gain an early advantage.

You'll experience quiet openings where the armies don't come into conflict with each other much, and you'll see wild skirmishes with lots of hitting and checkers being sent to the bar on every move.

Eventually though, the manoeuvring or mayhem ends and a recognisable pattern emerges. (These patterns define the middle game that I cover in Chapter 7.)

Defining the objectives

Check the Cheat Sheet at the front of the book for a reminder of the starting positions of your checkers. Notice that they're not particularly well distributed:

- ✔ All your checkers are on just four points.

- ✔ Ten checkers – a full two-thirds – are on two points – your 13-point, better known as the *mid-point*, and your 6-point.

- ✔ Two checkers are as far back as they can be in your opponent's home board and a long way from their nearest companions on the mid-point.

So, your first objective is to improve that opening distribution. Ideally, you want to advance your position while making it more difficult for your opponent to better his. So, in no particular order, I give you the opening objectives with some of the reasoning behind them:

- ✔ **Make a new point.** New points give your checkers places to land safely and at the same time block your opponent from moving as easily. A new point on either side of the board is a good thing, but preferably you want to make points in your home board.

- ✔ **Unstack your heavy points.** Having five checkers on a point is very inefficient. You need only two to own a point, so look to use the other three checkers to make new points somewhere else.

- ✔ **Activate your back checkers.** As they have the longest distance to travel to reach your home board, setting your backmost checkers on that journey as soon as possible makes sense.

What you're trying to achieve in the opening move helps determine the play you choose.

Introducing risk

Although it may not be immediately obvious, the opening is the time to take risks to improve your position. The reason is that at the start of the game your opponent only owns one point in his home board (his 6-point) so if he hits a blot of yours, you can re-enter that checker relatively easily.

Winning the Roll and Making the First Move

Because you can never start the game with a double – remember, you and your opponent each roll one dice and whoever rolls the higher number uses both numbers for their first play – the game can start with a total of 15 possible opening rolls. The next sections talk about how to play each one.

In normal money play, the choice of opening play quite often comes down to the player's style. The same is not true of match play, where the choice of opening play can be dictated by the match score. I discuss match play opening moves in Chapter 13.

Starting with the best

Five of the 15 possible rolls are much better than the other 10 and experts universally agree on how to play them, so they're called *forced opening moves*. Of course, no one physically forces you to play them, but you'll betray your amateur status if you don't. The next sections cover these five rolls.

Playing 31

The best possible opening roll is 31 because you can make your 5-point by playing 8/5, 6/5, as shown in Figure 4-1. Remember, your 5-point is one of the two most important points on the board, the other one being your opponent's 5-point.

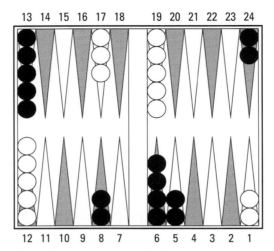

Figure 4-1: Playing an opening 31.

With your 5-point made, you have a good start towards making a *prime* – a row of consecutive points. If you can make your bar-point, you have a four-point prime from your 5-point to your 8-point, which is an extremely useful asset.

Playing 42

A roll of 42 is always played 8/4, 6/4. It has the advantage of creating a new home board point and also a point that can become part of a prime. Making your 4-point isn't quite as good as making your 5-point because of the gap between the 6-point and the 4-point.

Playing 53

You make a new home board point by moving 8/3, 6/3. Because of the gap between the points a 53 is slightly weaker than a 42 but a point is a point and you need to accept what the dice give you.

In the 1970s everybody played 13/8, 13/10 with an opening 53 because the 3-point was felt to be too deep a point to make so early. Then a guy named Jason Lester switched to making his 3-point and noticed the strength of the permanent asset. Pretty soon everyone switched to making the 3-point. I haven't seen anyone play 13/18, 13/10 for more than 20 years.

Playing 61

The last of the point-making rolls, you play 61 by moving 13/7, 8/7 and making your bar-point. Many beginners value the bar-point above the 5-point; however the bar-point is actually quite a bit weaker as an opening roll because the bar-point isn't a home board point and it doesn't make use of any of that stack of checkers on your 6-point. However, your bar-point immediately makes a three-point prime, which may well come in useful.

Playing 65

A roll of 65 provides you with an opportunity to escape one of your two back checkers to the safety of your mid-point by playing 24/18/13, as shown in Figure 4-2.

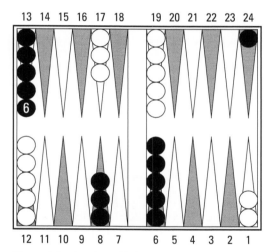

Figure 4-2: Running with 65.

I introduce a new diagram feature here to indicate how many checkers are on a point when there are more than five. The actual number of checkers is shown by a numeral within the top checker. Note the number 6 on the 13-point in Figure 4-2.

Escaping one of the back checkers is a good way to start the game and the strength of an opening 65 is sometimes underrated.

An opening 65 is known as *lover's leap*.

Stackin' 'em high

An old wives' tale says that you can't have more than five checkers on a point. As with many such tales, you won't find a grain of truth in it. If you so wish, you can have all 15 of your checkers on a single point, and I actually saw a player with all 15 checkers on his ace-point.

However, stacking lots of checkers on a small number of points is known as *building candlesticks*, and should be avoided because this leads to very inflexible positions.

Handling other opening moves

When you get to those rolls where you have a choice, things get a bit more difficult. The key is to keep the three key objectives in mind and find choices that help you achieve them. (See the 'Defining the objectives' section earlier in this chapter.)

The remaining rolls break down into three groups, which I explain in the following sections.

Splitting or slotting your roll

Playing 21, 41, or 51 leads to splitting or slotting:

- ✔ **Slotting** is exposing a checker within 6 pips of one of your opponent's checkers in the hope that if the shot is missed, you'll be able to cover and make a new point next turn.

- ✔ **Splitting** is separating your two back checkers with your first move.

You've nothing to choose between slotting and splitting. I nearly always slot because that's my style. Computers vote for splitting on certain moves but not others but the odds are very close. Try them both and see which choice you prefer.

Playing 21

A roll of 21 promotes either splitting or slotting. Figure 4-3 shows the slotting play of moving 13/11, 6/5.

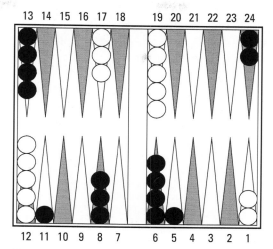

Figure 4-3: Slotting with 21.

This roll meets your opening objectives by unstacking both heavy points, and although it doesn't make a point, it starts the hugely valuable 5-point and provides a checker on the 11-point, which can be used to make the 5-point on your next turn.

The blot on the 11-point is known as a *builder*, which is a term that applies to a single blot on its own or any checkers on a point more than the two required to own the point. These checkers are available to build new points.

If White doesn't get a 4 next turn and hit the blot, then Black can almost certainly cover the blot and lay claim to her own 5-point.

The splitting play of 13/11, 24/23 with a 21 roll is shown in Figure 4-4.

This option unstacks one of the heavy points and also, albeit only in a minor way, starts one of the back checkers on its long journey home. Splitting the back checkers gives Black many more hitting numbers if White leaves a blot in his home or outer board. So this move also meets the objectives for an opening move. Which move is better is partly a matter of style. The slotting play tends to lead to very sharp games with lots of blots being hit; the splitting play leads to more defensive games. The difference resembles that between the Sicilian and Queen's Gambit openings in chess. Computers tell us that the slot is slightly better than the split, but I recommend going with the play you're more comfortable with. Try them both and see which you prefer.

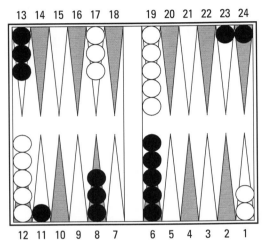

Figure 4-4: Splitting with 21.

You can also consider 13/10 or 24/21 as reasonable moves, but they don't play to the objectives as strongly as the two moves discussed here.

Playing 41

You can split or slot with 41, similar to what you can do with 21. You reject 13/8 because you don't want to make candlesticks – a few towers of many checkers – so you've the choice between slotting with 13/9, 6/5 and splitting with 13/9, 24/23.

Your personal preference is a major factor in your decision but arithmetic does come into it. The blot you leave on the 9-point after 13/9 is far more vulnerable than the blot on the 11-point in the equivalent 21 opening. White has 19 numbers to hit one of the two blots after 13/9, 6/5, which gives him slightly better than average odds, so making this move is quite a risky play. Computers definitely prefer 13/9, 24/23 but the choice is down to you.

Playing 51

With 51 the two choices are 13/8, 6/5 (slotting) and 13/8, 24/23 (splitting). The problem with 5s in the opening roll is that they don't really help much as you already own your 8-point. However, you must play what the dice give you and 13/8 is normally the best way to play a 5. 8/3 isn't really a sensible option.

24/18 is a play I've occasionally seen tried with 51 but the splitting and slotting options are both better.

Fixing on rolls with 6

The opening rolls of 62, 63, and 64 have always been the subject of great debates and the arguments continue.

Playing 62

If you took a time machine back 100 years, you'd see the normal 62 play 24/16, which runs one of the back checkers as far as possible. If you moved forward to the 1970s, the standard opening move with a 62 was to play 13/5, slotting the 5-point and starting a point there.

Eventually players worked out that the best approach is to boldly start your opponent's bar-point by moving 24/18 with the 6 and then to unstack the mid-point by moving 13/11, as shown in Figure 4-5.

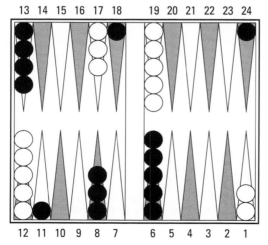

Figure 4-5: Playing an opening 62.

At first sight this move looks too bold, but consider: if White hits the blot on his bar-point, Black gets lots of return shots at White's blot (unless White made his bar-point with 61, 11, 33, or 66). And White may not hit Black's blot, in which case Black has an excellent chance to make White's bar-point next turn. Holding your opponent's bar-point is a vast improvement on holding his ace-point.

Playing 63

Exactly the same thinking as with playing 62 (see the preceding section) applies to the 63 roll. Playing 24/18, 13/10 has become more or less standard, although you still occasionally see the running play 24/15.

If you considered plays such as 13/7, 13/10 and 13/7, 24/21, take credit for seeing them, but realise that they're very weak in comparison to 24/18, 13/10 because they expose you to having both blots hit on your opponent's next turn. If you want to provoke a series of hits, do it on your opponent's bar-point, not your own. A hit on your bar point loses more pips in the race than a hit on your opponent's bar point.

Playing 64

The normal play is considered to be 24/18, 13/9, but two other plays come into serious consideration:

- ✔ The running play 24/14 is quite strong because it gets one of the back checkers very close to safety. White can hit the blot on the 14-point only with a 2. The same type of running play with 62 and 63 gives White more hitting numbers. The running play tends to lead to much simpler games than 24/18, 13/9.

- ✔ You can also make your 2-point with 8/2, 6/2. For years this move was scoffed at because the point was far too deep in your home board but computers have shown that this move is not as silly as it looks and is coming back into vogue – after all, a point is a point.

Rounding up the rest of the rolls

The rolls I talk about in these sections aren't the best rolls you can open with, but they still give you the advantage of making the first move, and it pays to know what to do with them.

Playing 32

If you get an opening roll of 32, you can play it 13/10/8, which is perfectly safe but, other than marginally unstacking your mid-point, does nothing to achieve the objectives I defined earlier in this chapter. Instead, try one of the much better moves here:

- 13/11, 13/10 brings two builders into range of your home board and is an aggressive play aimed at quickly making a prime.

- 24/21, 13/11 and 13/10, 24/22 strike a balance by creating a new builder but also advancing one of the two back men. (24/21, 13/11 is generally preferred to 13/10, 24/22.)

All three plays meet the objectives, so which you choose is a matter of style. Computers see very little difference between the plays. I leave it to you to make your own decision – so long as you never consider 13/8!

Playing 43

A roll of 43 is very similar to 32 and the three options are 13/9, 13/10; 13/9, 24/21; and 13/10, 24/20. And the same question arises: do you want to go aggressively for the prime or for one of the more balanced plays? Whereas with 32 the computers are undecided, they actually show a clear preference for 13/9, 13/10 with 43. Why this preference is so isn't clear and I know many players who swear by 13/10, 24/20, preferring to slot White's 5-point in the hope of making it next turn.

Playing 52

Rolling 52 isn't great. The two choices are the building play of 13/8, 13/11 or the splitting play of 13/8, 24/22, with virtually nothing to choose between them. You would, of course, reject 13/6 because it doesn't improve your position in any way.

Until five years ago, the split was completely out of vogue because of the fear that your opponent would then roll 33 or 55, both of which are very powerful responses. Obviously, your opponent may roll one of those doubles every so often, but if he doesn't the split is surprisingly effective.

Playing 54

Rolling 54 offers two choices: 13/9, 13/8, a building play; and 13/8, 24/20, a splitting play.

Time and computers have changed opinion on this roll. For many years, building was the universally accepted play but the critical importance of the two 5-points is now much better understood and the splitting play shown in Figure 4-6 is now recognised as being much the better choice.

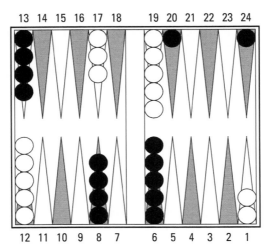

Figure 4-6: Splitting with 54.

Responding to the Opening Move

The first few moves of any game are vital because they dictate the course of play for many moves to come. So, you not only need to be prepared to make an important opening move yourself, which I cover in the previous sections, but also to respond to your opponent's first move, which I talk about now.

The objectives in responding are generally very similar to those in playing the opening roll – making a new point, unstacking your heavy points, and moving your backmost checkers – with the addition of two more:

✔ If your opponent has slotted his 5-point, for example, by playing 13/11, 6/5 with an opening 21, hitting that blot (if possible) is your priority.

✔ If you can hit one of his blots in the outer board, you should probably do so.

Destroying a slot

If your opponent has slotted his 5-point with his opening roll, your priority is to hit that blot and send it to the bar so that your opponent can't make his 5-point next turn.

In Figure 4-7, White's first move was the slotting play 13/11, 6/5, starting his own 5-point. You, as Black, now roll 31.

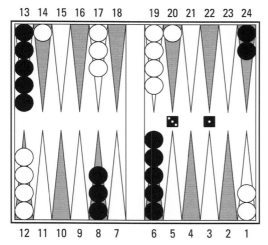

Figure 4-7: Destroying a slot.

Following the basic objectives, you may think that your best play is to make your own 5-point with 8/5, 6/5. But looking ahead, you can see that in all probability White will make his own 5-point next turn and then has the slightly better position because both sides have their 5-points but he's also moved some of his other checkers into good positions.

Playing 24/20* and sending the blot to the bar is a much better play for three very positive reasons:

✔ White's checker is on the bar.

✔ Black's checker is on White's 5-point, increasing the likelihood that Black can make that point.

✔ Black takes the lead in the race because White's hit blot must travel all the way around the board again.

Much of backgammon involves balancing risks and rewards. In this play, the rewards are high and the risks minimal (other than not making your own 5-point), so 24/20* is the obvious play.

In Figure 4-8, White opened with 54, played 13/8, 24/20. As Black, you can avoid the battle and quietly play 24/21 with your 21 roll, but battles (in the main) aren't won by staying in the trenches. You must fight for your 5-point and play 13/11, 6/5*.

This is much better than 8/5* because one of the stack of checkers on the 13-point is developed into a new and useful position. For example, it can be used to cover the blot on the 5-point next turn with a 6.

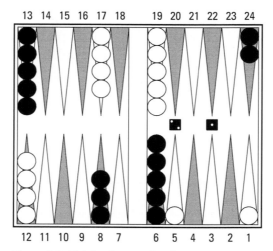

Figure 4-8: Fighting for your 5-point.

You may then fight over your 5-point. Sometimes you'll be victorious and at other times your opponent will triumph, but these skirmishes are the very nature of the game.

If you play non-aggressively at the beginning of the game, you're more likely to end up having the inferior position. One of backgammon's oldest adages is 'When in doubt, hit'.

Sometimes the decision is more difficult as in the situation shown in Figure 4-9. White played his opening 62 by moving

24/18, 13/11. You roll 31. Using the 1 to hit White's blot by moving 8/7* and playing 13/10 or 24/21 with the 3 may look like the best option – but is a mistake.

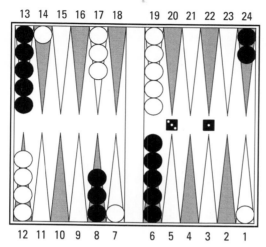

Figure 4-9: Hitting incorrectly.

The 5-point is so important that passing up the hit in favour of making your 5-point with 8/5, 6/5 is the most sensible play.

To show that backgammon can be a game of fine detail, consider what you can do if you roll 42 instead of 31 – hit or make your 4-point? If you choose to make your 4-point in this situation, you're making a very small mistake, but a mistake nonetheless. Making your 4-point doesn't give you the same strength of position that making your 5-point does, so hitting instead is the slightly better play. Tricky game, backgammon!

Gaining tempo with a hit

Taking away half your opponent's roll by hitting a blot is known as *gaining a tempo*. Your opponent is forced to spend half his roll entering from the bar and so maybe won't be able to do anything constructive elsewhere on the board – unless he rolls a double.

White played his opening roll of 62 by moving 24/18, 13/11. How to play your 54 responding roll is the issue shown in Figure 4-10.

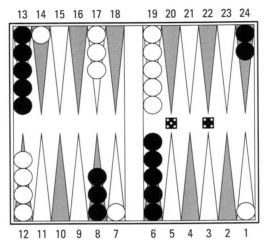

Figure 4-10: Playing an awkward 54.

No matter what you play, you leave a blot for White to shoot at somewhere on the board. If that's the case, then why not take away half of White's next roll by hitting his blot? It may look odd, at least at first, but the correct play is 6/1*, 24/20. This move starts to make an anchor on your opponent's 5-point, and forces White to use half of his next roll (excepting doubles) to enter from the bar, which makes it difficult for him to make a new point on his next roll.

Changing Priorities

Your choice of response obviously must take into account your opponent's first move. Here are a few guidelines:

- ✔ If there's a blot to be hit, hit it! (with the odd exception, as I explain in the preceding section).

- ✔ If your opponent has made a home board point and you can't make one yourself, split the back checkers if you can.

✔ If your opponent has escaped a back checker with a roll like 65, then split the back checkers unless you can make a home board point.

✔ After your opponent has made a new home board point, avoid slotting – doing so is too risky now.

Consider the situation in Figure 4-11 in which White opened with a 42 by making his 4-point.

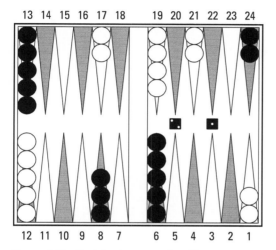

Figure 4-11: Replying to an opening 42.

You, as Black, now roll 21. If this move were the first one of the game, you could choose between splitting (13/11, 24/23) and slotting (13/11, 6/5). But because White has a second home board point which limits Black's re-entry from the bar, the slotting play that exposes a blot to a direct hit is too dangerous. The splitting play is mandatory and Black must play 13/11, 24/23. This move brings a useful builder into the outer board and diversifies the rear checkers. You still have two blots, but White needs both die to hit the blot on your 11-point.

When your opponent uses the spare checker on his 8-point to make a new home board point, normally your correct response is to split your back checkers. Your opponent can't then use one of the two remaining checkers on the 8-point to make another home point (with a 31 next turn, for example) without leaving the last checker on the 8-point exposed to a direct shot from you.

Dealing with Doubles

One roll – or six rolls, actually – that can give you an early advantage is doubles. You can often do two good things with your four moves rather than just one – and you should at least try.

The fact that you get four moves instead of two is a big advantage. The majority of the time you can use doubles to make two new points, which is great progress.

Most doubles play well in the opening with the exception of double 5 which plays a bit awkwardly because of how the checkers are set up at the start of the game.

Figure 4-12 shows the position after White opens with a 61 and makes his bar-point, and Black has a 44 to play.

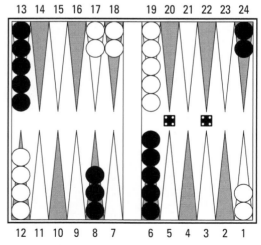

Figure 4-12: Replying with 44 – a great roll.

You can run your two backmost checkers all the way to the 16-point by playing 24/16(2). Alternatively, you can make your own 5-point by playing 13/5(2). Both these moves accomplish one good thing – making a new point – but you can do better.

With two 4s, you can play 24/20(2), taking possession of your opponent's 5-point (notice that the 5-point keeps reappearing as a strategic position). With the other two 4s, you play 13/9(2), which unstacks the heavy mid-point and makes a new outer board point.

It may seem that 8/4(2) would be a better use of those last two 4s but actually 13/9(2) gives a better distribution of the checkers and doesn't leave a blot exposed on the 8-point.

Part II

Handling the Middle Game

The 5th Wave

By Rich Tennant

'Him? That's me brother-in-law. Thought we could use a time keeper. Hope you don't mind.'

In this part . . .

Welcome to Part II, where I unlock the mysterious complexities of the middle game. In plain English I explain doubling, probably the most difficult area of backgammon. However, with the chapters in this part, you'll be a confident player in no time!

Chapter 5

Upping the Stakes by Doubling

*I*f you could travel back in time to New York in the early 1920s, life in general would be exciting indeed, except in the area of games playing. Backgammon was being played as it had been for thousands of years, which presented two big problems:

✔ The games took too long.

✔ The gambling element wasn't very exciting.

Both of these problems disappeared at a stroke around 1926. Somewhere in one of the New York gaming clubs a genius, or it may have been a group of them, conceived the idea of being able to double the stakes during a game. Backgammon was changed forever. Without that invention, the game may have died a sorry death 80 years ago.

In this chapter I explain the basic concepts of doubling and show you how to deal with simple doubling decisions. I also establish a few basic doubling principles that stand you in good stead for the rest of your backgammon career.

Sadly, you can't understand doubling without doing some arithmetic, so dust off your pencil and prepare to do a few sums!

This chapter isn't easy and you may need to read it a few times before you become comfortable with the content.

Understanding the Basics of Doubling

You're playing a game (and it could be any game) and your opponent says to you, 'I think I'm winning this game, why don't we double the stakes?' In backgammon, such a question is common because a player who feels that she has a sufficient advantage can propose doubling the stakes. The stakes can be anything from money to matchsticks.

Most people's initial reaction to such a proposition is to say, 'Why should I risk losing twice as much money? No, thank you very much.' If you could play on for the original stake that would be fine, but that's not how doubling works in backgammon. Once your opponent offers a double, you must give up the game, pay the agreed stake, and start another game, or continue playing for double the original stake.

With the addition of the doubling cube, you don't have to win the race to win the game; all you need to do is get your opponent to decline a double. Only if you double and your opponent accepts, do you have to get to the finish line first to be victorious.

In a game you may make up to 30 decisions about how to move your checkers, but you're likely to make only two or three doubling of decisions, so taking the time to get them right is worth it. As Paul Magriel said, in his 1976 book *Backgammon*, 'Good checker play will never compensate for serious errors of judgement in doubling.'

Introducing the doubling cube and counting by doubles

The *doubling cube* – the rather odd die with the numbers 2, 4, 8, 16, 32, and 64 on its six sides – has the job of showing what the current stake is and who last accepted a double. Figure 5-1 shows a typical doubling cube, which is often called simply *the cube*.

Figure 5-1: The odd die that comes with your backgammon set is known as the doubling cube or 'the cube'.

At the start of the game, you position the cube so that the 64, which equates to 1 because the cube doesn't have a 1, is on top and placed near the centre of the board. Normally the cube is off to one side as shown in the diagrams, but some boards have a slot in the centre of the bar to hold the doubling cube.

From here on the figures show the position of the doubling cube. If no double has been offered and accepted, the cube shows a value of 64 and sits in the centre on the right-hand side of the board. If Black owns the cube, meaning that he has accepted a double, the cube is displayed on his side of the board with the appropriate value – and the same for White.

Each game starts with a stake of one point. If you win a game without any doubles, you gain one point and win the basic stake.

You don't have a limit to the number of times you can offer a double in one game. Between two good players, the doubling cube rarely shows more than 8 in a game and most games finish with the cube on 1, 2, or 4. But note that 'rarely' is not the same as 'never' and occasionally a 32, 64, or even a 128 double creeps in (just because the cube stops at 64 doesn't mean you can't double beyond 64!).

If the cube value goes beyond 64, you and your opponent must remember its value – you've no way of physically showing 128 and above.

An American master, who shall remain nameless, managed to lose $30,000 in a single game a couple of years ago. Admittedly he was playing in a chouette, the multi-player version of the game, but even so, when the nominal stake is $100 – as it was in this particular game – $30,000 is quite a lot of money.

Be sure that you know what you're doing when the cube rises to high levels and, even more importantly, make sure that you can pay up if you lose!

Presenting the procedure

When you want to offer a double, you do so when you take your turn and you haven't yet rolled the dice. You turn the doubling cube to the next higher value and say, 'I double'. (If this double is the first one of the game, you turn the cube to 2.) A double must always take the cube to the next higher value; from 1 to 2, 2 to 4, 4 to 8, and so on.

A player offered a double may refuse, in which case he concedes the game, is down one point, and pays the original stake. Otherwise he must accept the double and play on for the new, higher stake of two points and double the original stake.

Help! What's that furry creature on the board?

The rule of the doubling cube only rising by one level has one exception. What do you do if your opponent doubles you and you believe that you're the favourite in the position?

The answer is that you *beaver* the double. When you beaver you raise the value of the doubling cube an extra level and *keep it on your side of the board*. For example, if your opponent doubles you to 2 and you believe that you're favourite, you beaver to 4.

If your opponent thinks she was still right and your beaver is wrong, she raccoons the beaver to 8. The cube still stays on your side of the board. If you think her raccoon is wrong, you can aardvark it to 16! At this point, we run out of furry animals.

Beavers are an optional extra and must be agreed by both players before play commences. While beavers are relatively common, raccoons are rare, and aardvarks virtually extinct.

I suggest not playing beavers until you've played backgammon for quite a while. They're fun but can be financially damaging if you're inexperienced.

Protocol dictates that when you accept a double, you say 'I take' or just 'take' and you place the cube on your side of the board with the new value on the uppermost face. Once you own the cube, only you may make the next double.

Accepting a double is known as a *take*. Declining a double is known as a *drop* or a *pass*. Subsequent doubles in the same game are called *redoubles*.

A player who refuses a redouble must pay the number of points at stake prior to the redouble. Otherwise he becomes the new owner of the cube and the game continues at twice the previous stake.

Estimating Your Chances

Doubling is largely about playing the odds. You have to know your chances of winning the game in order to offer or respond to a double.

So the first question to address is how to determine who is actually winning at any point during a game of backgammon. And, although you have to take many positional considerations into account, at its heart backgammon is a race, and the majority of the time, the player winning the race is winning the game.

Counting pips to see who's ahead

To work out who's winning the race you do a pip count. Put simply, a *pip count* is a tally of the number of dice pips you need to throw in order to bear off your checkers. You do the same for your opponent and compare the two pip counts to see who is winning.

To calculate a pip count, use the following steps. And, as we may as well begin at the beginning, the following shows how to figure the pip count for the starting position. Figure 5-2 shows the final tally.

1. **Assign a value to each point equal to its designation from your point of view.**

   So, the value of your 6-point is 6, your 8-point is 8, your mid-point is 13, and your opponent's ace-point is 24.

2. Multiply the number of checkers on each point by the value of the point.

So, at the start of the game, your numbers look like as follows:

- $5 \times 6 = 30$ for the checkers on your 6-point
- $3 \times 8 = 24$ for the checkers on your 8-point
- $5 \times 13 = 65$ for the checkers on your mid-point
- $2 \times 24 = 48$ for the checkers on your opponent's 1-point

3. Add the accumulated totals.

The pip count in the starting position is: $30 + 24 + 65 + 48 = 167$.

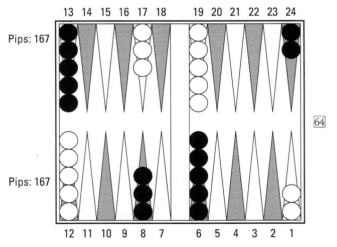

Figure 5-2: Counting pips at the start.

If you don't like doing arithmetic in your head, doing pip counts may seem daunting at first, but it becomes much easier with practice and even players who aren't particularly good at arithmetic soon grasp the idea. And, normally each player's count gets smaller than the initial 167 as the game progresses, – at least you hope it does!

From here on, I show the pip count on every subsequent diagram – White's pip count in the upper left-hand corner of the diagram and Black's in the lower left-hand corner, as shown in Figure 5-2.

You don't do a pip count every time you take your turn to play. You always need to have a general idea about who is ahead because that information influences your game plan, but you normally do a pip count for one of two specific reasons:

✔ Your choice of play depends directly on who leads in the race.

✔ You need to make a decision about doubling, to offer a double or to accept or refuse your opponent's double.

Deciding on a double is by far the most common reason to do a pip count.

Applying the 25 per cent rule

Accepting doubling the stakes when you're losing, which is likely to be the only time you're offered a double, seems to go against the grain. But consider two players, A and B, playing four games of backgammon:

✔ In the first scenario, Player A doubles Player B in each of the four games. Player B refuses all four doubles and is therefore down four points (–4).

✔ In the second scenario, Player A doubles Player B in each game but this time Player B accepts the doubles. He goes on to lose three games but wins the fourth game. He loses two points in each of the games he loses (–6) and wins two points in the game he wins (+2). His net result is –4 points, which is the same outcome as in the first scenario.

So, the prime rule of doubling, known as *the 25 per cent rule*, is: if you can expect to win 25 per cent of the time from the position you're in, you can (and should) accept a double.

The 25 per cent rule is what makes backgammon so exciting. You accept a double when you're in a position in which you're clearly the underdog, and you can't get a better feeling than turning the game around and winning it.

Doubling and the 25 per cent rule change the very nature of the game: you don't have to get to the end of a game and be the first to bear off all your checkers to win a game. All you need to do is get to a point where you've a greater than 75 per cent chance to win the game, offer your opponent a double, and she has to drop (although she may erroneously take).

If you're having trouble with the thought of all the arithmetic, keep in mind that the bottom line when it comes to taking or refusing a double is to ask yourself whether you can expect to win approximately once in four times in the same situation. If your answer is yes, then you have a take. I know that until you've played at least some backgammon you can't possibly expect to answer this question accurately but the more you play the easier it becomes.

Improving your odds by owning the cube

Owning the cube is worth something. The longer a game has to go (and hence the more time you have to turn things round), the more valuable that ownership becomes.

Owning the cube is generally reckoned to be worth an additional 10 per cent of winning chances. So, 10 per cent of 25 per cent – the point at which you accept a double – is 2.5 per cent so, rather than needing exactly 25 per cent chances to take, the more general figure used by the majority of players is the range 22 per cent to 23 per cent. (Check the earlier section 'Counting pips to see who's ahead' for help in determining what your chances are.)

Answering the Three Key Questions about Doubling

Doubling is by far the most difficult area of backgammon to master, so don't worry if you're not at all clear on the concept yet. I've been playing for 30 years and I'm still discovering new things about doubling every time I play.

The three key questions with regard to doubling are:

✔ When should you double?

✔ When should you redouble?

✔ When should you take a double and when should you drop a double?

The answers to each of these questions could fill a book. For now I offer a few broad answers. In percentage terms, the answers are:

✔ You need to be about a 66 per cent favourite (or better) to win the game in order to offer a double.

✔ You need to be close to a 70 per cent favourite to redouble.

✔ You need to have a 22 to 25 per cent chance of winning to accept a double or a redouble. If your chances are less than that, refuse the double.

Why the difference between doubling and redoubling? Quite simply, when you offer an initial double both players have access to the cube. When you redouble you give away something you own exclusively – as you accepted the initial double, the doubling cube is in your possession and you're the only one who can redouble. If you offer a redouble and your opponent accepts it, she then owns the cube. Therefore you need to be in a slightly stronger position to redouble than to give an initial double.

Offering a double

For many years after doubling was introduced, the concept of doing a pip count was unknown and players managed by approximation. In the 1970s, when the game experienced a huge surge in popularity, some of the young United States players who came into the game began to work out formulae to assist with doubling. These have been refined to a point where you now have highly sophisticated formulae available, if you wish to use them. The reason that all these formulae work is that a 10 per cent lead in the race roughly equates to having a 75 per cent chance to win the game.

✔ The simplest formula says that if your lead in the race is 10 per cent, you're far enough ahead to double and your opponent still has enough chances to be able to take.

As an example, if your pip count is 90 and your opponent's is 99, you're 10 per cent ahead (10 per cent of 90 is 10/100 × 90 = 9) and you should double and your opponent should take (see the previous bullet point).

✔ A more refined estimation goes as follows:

- If you lead in the pip count by 8 per cent or more, you should double but not redouble.

- If you lead in the pip count by 9 per cent or more, you should both double and redouble.

  Notice that you need a slightly bigger advantage to redouble rather than offer an initial double, reflecting the fact that owning the cube is worth something. (See the 'Improving your odds by owning the cube' section earlier in this chapter.)

- If you're doubled then you can take provided you're no more than 12 per cent behind.

This formula works well for most races where the pip counts are 30 or above. When the game reaches the very end, you need to consider additional factors such as the distribution of the checkers and the number of checkers already borne off.

Figure 5-3 shows a position from which to put the formula into practice.

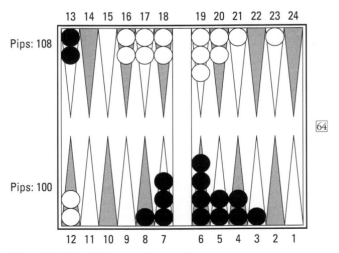

Figure 5-3: Practising your pip-counting.

As you work out the pip counts for both players, you discover that Black's pip count is 100 and White's is 108. Black's lead is 8 pips, which is also 8 per cent. The formula says that Black should double but that he shouldn't redouble if he already owns the doubling cube. White trails by less than 12 per cent so White can take the double.

Using the formulae takes the anxiety out of the decision-making process.

Looking at end-game doubling decisions

Getting to grips with doubling is probably the most difficult thing to do in backgammon but if you persevere you can soon get to grips with it.

I start off with doubling examples from the end game when few checkers are left on the board so you can calculate the outcome of the game and confirm the accuracy of the doubling decisions.

Figure 5-4 shows a situation to which you can apply the 25 per cent rule. And, what could be simpler? It's Black's turn and he's ready to win the game on his next roll. But, wait a minute! What happens if he rolls 21? Then he fails to bear off his last checker and White wins the game. Unlucky maybe, but this situation happens twice in every 36 games because two ways to roll 12 exist out of 36 possible two-dice rolls. So, Black has a 94 per cent chance of winning the game.

Note: I consistently evaluate an outcome in terms of 36 games because 36 is the number of possible rolls of two dice. (See the Cheat Sheet at the front of the book for the complete dice table.)

With the doubling cube in play, Black can offer White a double, and White should decline as she has barely a 6 per cent chance of winning, which is nowhere near the 25 per cent she needs in order to take a double. Therefore, Black always wins from this position provided he has access to the doubling cube.

One of the key impacts of the cube is that it reduces the element of luck.

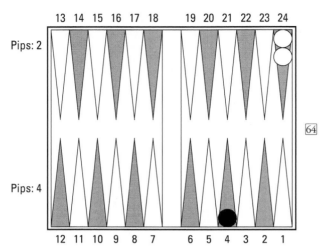

Figure 5-4: An easy decision.

Figure 5-5 shows a slight variation in the position.

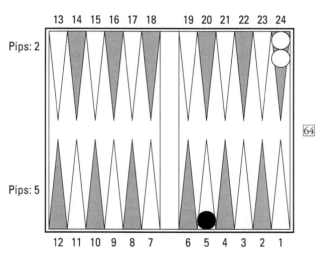

Figure 5-5: Still a drop.

Black loses only when he rolls 11, 12, 21, 13, 31. Thus he wins 31 out of 36 times or 86.1 per cent of the time. Again, in this position Black should double, and White should drop because she has less than a 25 per cent chance of winning. So Black wins the point and the stake.

However, the simple addition of just one more checker changes things considerably, as shown in Figure 5-6.

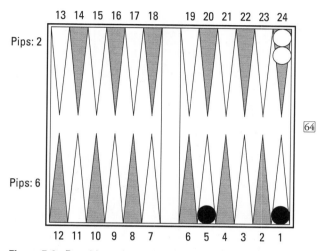

Figure 5-6: Reaching take territory.

Now Black can win only with 23 out of a possible 36 rolls. At this point, if Black offers a double, White is going to take it. Note that because this roll is effectively the last one of the game, Black should double with any advantage at all – even 51 per cent would be enough.

Instead of looking at percentages this time, I'm going to look at the possible outcome of 36 games in terms of points won or lost. This is an alternative way of looking at things which some people find more comfortable:

In 36 games:

- ✔ If White drops, she loses $36 \times (-1) = -36$
- ✔ If White takes, she loses $23 \times (-2) = -46$
  but wins $13 \times (+2) = +26$
  for a net loss of -20

As White is better off taking than dropping, she must accept the double. On the last roll of the game, doubling with any advantage at all is correct and if the opponent has 25 per cent winning chances, she'll take. The bear-off position with the smallest possible advantage is shown in Figure 5-7.

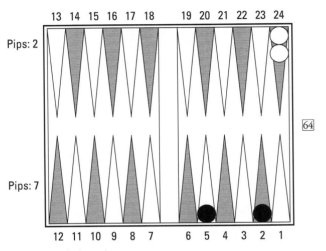

Figure 5-7: A tiny advantage.

Here, Black is only a 19/36 (52.8 per cent) favourite yet offering a double is still correct. White has an easy take.

Last-roll positions are relatively straightforward and easy to calculate. But if you're not certain to win or lose on your next roll, that changes things. Take Black's position in Figure 5-8, for example.

Analysing this situation requires a little work to get to the right answer. Don't worry, backgammon isn't all arithmetic by any means, but in the end game you can use it to your advantage. Also, and critically, you don't have to do this arithmetic every time you play.

In Figure 5-8, Black is in place to win on his next roll unless he rolls a 1. That means he wins 25/36 (69 per cent) of the time on his roll so it certainly looks as if he should double.

What about White – should she take or drop? At first glance, she needs to drop the double because even when she does get to roll she wins just 69 per cent of the time herself, as she's in the same situation as Black and needs to not roll a 1.

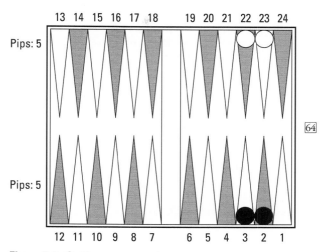

Figure 5-8: Getting more complex.

The probability of two events occurring is the product of the two percentages so in this case White's overall chances of winning are therefore 31 per cent (Black misses) × 69 per cent (White doesn't miss), which is only 21 per cent – well below the 25 per cent benchmark.

But this calculation overlooks a vital factor. Whenever Black fails to bear off his two checkers White will *redouble* to 4 before she rolls because now she is the one who is going to win 69 per cent of the time on her next roll. Although White only wins 21 per cent of the time overall, when she does win she wins 4 points rather than 2. That difference is enough to turn what would be a drop into a take.

Remembering Reference Positions

Worried by all these numbers? Don't be, help is at hand! I know lots of brilliant backgammon players who wouldn't know a percentage if they met one. They're brilliant because they have a huge store of reference positions that they use constantly when playing and they add to that store every time they play. Elephants would be superb backgammon players!

Although apparently a simple game of calculating the odds, in backgammon you can rarely arrive at the right answer through calculation alone.

With many board games, types of positions constantly recur. In backgammon, you see types of positions again and again with slight variations in the details. You make use of these reference positions by recognising the recurring pattern. *Reference positions* are situations that you remember from previous games. You can apply the correct doubling action and/or playing strategy from the earlier instance to other, similar positions. Any good player has a huge library of reference positions in his memory and uses pattern recognition to access that reference library.

Fortunately, as you become more experienced, you rely much more on reference positions than you do on calculations. Hurray! You become familiar with when to double, redouble, and take or drop because types of positions constantly repeat.

Chapter 6

Progressing to Advanced Doubling

In This Chapter

▶ Understanding the principles of doubling

▶ Deciding whether your position is stable

▶ Including gammons in your calculations

▶ Playing the mind game

▶ Knowing when your position is too good to redouble

*A*lthough doubling has been around for the best part of eighty years, only in the last twenty have players really come to understand the complexities and subtleties of handling the doubling cube.

When backgammon started its great revival in the mid-1960s, it's safe to say that even most of the top players of the time didn't use the cube very well.

Georges Mabardi, one of the top players in the 1920s, stated not long after the invention of doubling, 'If two absolutely perfect players engaged in a match, there would never be an accepted double.' Close but no cigar, Georges!

Doubling is undoubtedly the most difficult part of backgammon so here I explore it more deeply and give you additional guidelines that help you make doubling decisions.

Good Principles Make Good Doubles

Although you can classify backgammon games into certain types, and I do just that in Chapter 8, so many possible backgammon positions exist that you can't be expected to work things out from basic rules on every turn. So you need good guidelines to use when giving and taking (or dropping) doubles.

Every roll is a new cube decision. Just because you didn't double last turn doesn't mean you shouldn't double this time. Assuming that you have access to the cube, *always* think about the doubling cube before you roll your dice.

The next sections cover the three key principles to consider before doubling – where you are in the race, how well you're positioned on the board, and what kind of threat you pose.

The rule: if you stand better in at least two of these three elements, you need to at least consider doubling.

Checking your position in the race

Remember that backgammon is essentially a race, so being ahead is a good thing.

Chapter 5 explains how to do a pip count to see whether you or your opponent is winning the race. Pop back to that chapter if you need a refresher.

Inspecting your structure

Many elements contribute to the strengths and weaknesses of a backgammon position. Following is a list of the essential elements to consider for both yourself and your opponent:

- **Number of home board points.** The more home board points you have, the stronger your position.

✔ **Whether you have a prime or a potential prime.** The game is in your favour if you have or can create a prime with opponent checkers trapped behind it.

✔ **Whether you have an anchor in your opponent's home board or on his bar-point.** An anchor in your opponent's home board is an asset because it gives you a place to enter from the bar and it stops your opponent blitzing you off the board. The bar-point anchor is slightly weaker but still a good asset.

✔ **Whether you have blots.** Having blots that your opponent can hit is a weakness. Conversely, if he has vulnerable blots, that's a positive for you.

✔ **How well connected your checkers are.** Of course, I'm not talking about knowing the rich and famous. This sort of connectedness is more about making sure that your checkers have open lines of communication. If you have three checkers deep in your opponent's home board and the other twelve in your home board, your position is fairly weak. Ideally you want to have enough bases so that your checkers, particularly on your opponent's side of the board, can communicate with each other.

You need to make a judgement on these elements and decide who has the better structure. Once again, practice makes perfect – or at least sets you on the road to perfection.

Evaluating threats

Evaluating threats is the key to good doubling. A *threat* is an action you may be able to take on your next roll that would damage your opponent's position. You need to make the evaluation for both yourself and your opponent.

Examples of threats include the possibility of:

✔ Hitting an opponent's blot(s)

✔ Making a new point(s)

✔ Completing or extending a prime

✔ Bringing your last checker into your home board safely

Putting the principles into practice

Time to put yourself to the test! I recommend that you make your own decision on each position before you read the text that comes after it. In each position, you're Black.

In Figure 6-1 Black has a slight edge in the race but not enough to be conclusive. In terms of structure, the two sides are virtually identical, both with perfect home boards. But Black most certainly presents a threat. Any 6 (you have 17 of them to contend with – check the dice table on the Cheat Sheet at the front of the book) virtually guarantees the win for Black, and 44 and 55 are good rolls as well. As Black, you're ahead in two elements, so you must certainly double.

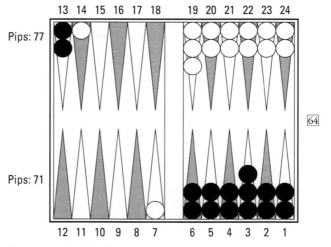

Figure 6-1: Leading in 2 out of 3 elements.

Now, should White take? Yes, because he has reasonable racing chances, and as Black you have to play carefully with non-hitting rolls so that you don't leave a blot yourself. (If you roll 52, for example, play 6/1, 6/4.) White is unlikely to lose a gammon and can probably win 25 per cent of the time.

In Figure 6-2, the boot is on the other foot and White is offering you a double. Do you accept? Proceeding logically you look at all three elements:

✔ **Race:** White is 18 pips ahead (a checker on the bar is counted as 25 pips) – significant advantage to White.

✔ **Position:** White owns three points in his home board, Black has one. Structural advantage to White.

✔ **Threats:** White has the potential for a powerful attack because Black has no anchor. White can build a prime (he already has 3 points of a potential prime – his 6-point, 5-point, and 3-point, as well as the checker on his bar-point). Black has a blot on his 10-point.

Things aren't looking good for Black. White is ahead in all three elements and has a powerhouse double. The double is so powerful that Black should be grateful to drop and get on to the next game.

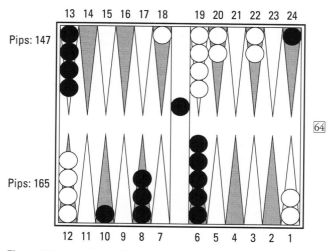

Figure 6-2: Leading in all three.

Judging Volatility and Looking for Market Losers

Some backgammon positions are inherently *stable*, meaning that not much is going to change in the next two rolls. Others are extremely *unstable*, that is, subject to significant and immediate change. An unstable position is known as *volatile*, a stable one as *non-volatile*. Table 6-1 shows elements of both types.

Table 6-1	Characteristics of Stable and Volatile Positions	
Stable/Non-volatile	**Unstable/Volatile**	
You have no blots.	One or more blots are vulnerable to direct hits.	
You have an anchor.	You don't have an anchor.	
The position won't change much by your next turn.	The position is likely to undergo significant change by your next turn.	

Figure 6-3 shows an example of a highly volatile position. After Black's next roll, White may well have two checkers on the bar and a weak position.

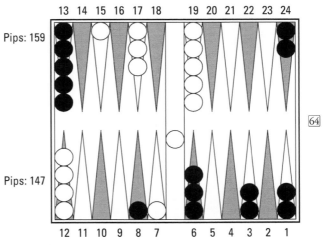

Figure 6-3: A volatile situation.

Contrast this position with that shown in Figure 6-4, where not much is going to happen for the next few rolls unless one player or the other rolls 44, 55, or 66. Otherwise, both sides will carefully manoeuvre their checkers and try to improve their positions.

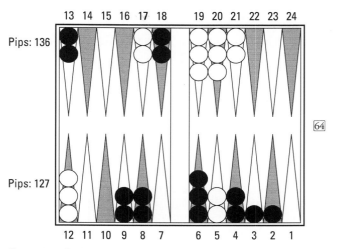

Figure 6-4: Both sides are quite stable.

In this position, no one is likely to double in the next few rolls. The exact opposite is true of the previous position, which demands an immediate double from Black.

The difference between the two positions is that the first one has market-losing sequences and the second one doesn't. A *market-losing sequence* is a situation in which your opponent has a take if you double this roll but won't be able to take a double after your next roll and his subsequent roll.

One of the keys to winning backgammon is to double when you have a strong threat, not after you've executed that threat perfectly. Remember, your opponent has to have some chance of winning in order to take your double. Winning just one point when you may have won four (via a doubled gammon) won't make you rich, or leave you satisfied.

Of course, sometimes you double and your opponent turns the game around and wins it. You just develop the knack of living with that possibility. If certainty is what you seek, backgammon is probably not for you. If, however, you want excitement, you're playing the right game!

Unless you have at least one opportunity for a market-losing sequence, you're certainly wrong to double. Figure 6-4 in the preceding section is an excellent example of positions from which neither side should double.

Accommodating Gammons

Life would be simple if it weren't for gammons. You lose a gammon when you fail to bear off any of your checkers before your opponent has taken all his off.

When I explained the 25 per cent rule for taking in Chapter 5 I didn't consider gammons. I'm now going to look at the impact of gammons on doubling. This subject is pretty tricky stuff, so please be patient and maybe read this section a couple of times to make sure that you understand the principles involved.

When you lose a gammon, you lose twice the stake and twice the value of the doubling cube – if the cube is on 2, you lose four points.

To demonstrate the impact of losing gammons, I look at a group of 100 games:

✔ In the first scenario, Black takes White's double to 2, wins 25 games but loses 75 games. Her net score is +50 (25 games won times 2) minus 150 (75 games lost times 2) for a net result of –100, which is exactly the same as if she'd dropped White's double in all 100 games.

The 25 per cent rule, which I explain in Chapter 5 and which dictates that you take a double if you have a 25 per cent chance of winning, holds true.

✔ In the second scenario, Black again takes White's double to 2, wins 25 games, loses 75 games but 10 of these losses are gammons. Her net score is $(25 \times 2) + (65 \times -2) + (10 \times -4) = -120$. Now she is worse off by taking the double in the initial position and therefore she should drop the double.

In any single game, if you accept a double and win the game, you show a profit of 4 points because you go from –2 – the points you would've lost – to +2 – the points you win. If you take a double and lose a gammon, you go from –2 to –4 for an additional loss of –2.

Winning a doubled game is twice as valuable as losing a gammon.

Consider:

> If you take and lose a gammon = –4
>
> If you take and lose a single = –2
>
> If you take and win a single = +2

So you need to convert one single loss to a single win (a gain of 4 points) to compensate for converting two single losses into gammon losses (a loss of 4 points).

The following gives you a basic rule for adjusting for gammons: take the percentage of gammons you expect to lose, divide that figure by 2 and add it to the basic 25 per cent take point. This rule clearly shows that with a gammon at risk, you need better chances to take a double.

The big question is how you know how often you'll lose a gammon from any given position. Sadly, no silver bullet exists. You have to develop your knowledge through studying and playing experience, and becoming comfortable with your own judgement may take time. Being able to answer this question is just another element of your backgammon reference library that you build throughout your playing career.

All this information may be quite daunting but after you've played for a few months, you get a good understanding of gammons. Most players don't make exact calculations over the board – there may not be time – they tend to rely on their reference library and so should you.

In the second scenario in the preceding list, as Black you expect that 10 per cent of your losses will be gammons. Divide that figure by 2 to get 5 per cent. Add that to 25 per cent and you get your new take point of 30 per cent. To quickly check the arithmetic:

In 100 games, you take a double to 2 every time. By the odds, you win 30 games (+60), lose 60 single games (–120) and 10 gammons (–40). So your win/loss equation looks like: 60 – 120 – 40 = –100, which is the same result you get if you drop the initial double every time.

So the sums are right.

Certain types of game – particularly blitzes, which I explain in Chapter 8 – lead to a high percentage of gammons.

Figure 6-5 shows the position after White played his opening roll of 63 by moving 24/18, 13/10. Black responded with 55 and correctly played 8/3(2), 6/1(2)*. White then rolled 61 and stayed on the bar.

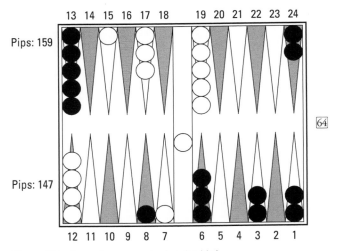

Figure 6-5: An early game-winning double!

Despite the game being only two moves old, Black has a powerful double that White must drop! White will lose a high percentage of gammons (about 40 per cent, from my reference library) from this position.

That means (using our formula) that he needs 25 (the basic take point) + 40/2 = 20 (the gammon percentage divided by 2) = 45 per cent winning chances to take. Although he's close, he can't quite do it so must drop your double – this point is the easiest (and quickest) point you'll win at backgammon!

Applying the Jacoby rule in money games

Oswald Jacoby, the great US bridge and backgammon player, introduced a rule named in his honour. The *Jacoby rule* states that a gammon cannot be won by either player unless the doubling cube has been offered and accepted during the course of the game. This rule only applies to money games and is never used in tournament backgammon.

This rule exists to speed up the game and to stop players taking up a lot of time finishing one-sided games. A sure-to-win player has to just take her one point and move on to the next game.

Of course, sometimes a player doubles to take her 'sure' point, and lo and behold, their opponent takes! So the doubling player wins a gammon and four points instead of just one – sometimes Christmas does come early!

Applying Psychology

In the examples and scenarios I assume that all the players are playing rationally and making sensible doubling decisions based on their knowledge of the game. I also assume that they have a well-balanced temperament and are never influenced by the vagaries of the dice. If these assumptions were always true, backgammon wouldn't be the wonderful, exciting game that it is. Luckily human beings come in all shapes, sizes, and temperaments and so if you play long enough you see all manner of weird and wonderful plays and doubling decisions.

The huge swing of fortune you experience when a poker player fills an inside straight with her final card is nothing compared to what can happen in backgammon. You can be calmly winning a gammon when your opponent rolls 16 from the bar, hits a blot, and suddenly he ends up winning the gammon. Instead of winning four points, you lose four points. A calm personality is necessary to merely raise an eyebrow when that sort of thing happens.

Temper or frustration or even recklessness gets the better of every player at some point. The next sections talk about typical emotional reactions.

Steaming

Most players behave reasonably at the start of a session but, as the evening wears on and one piece of bad luck follows another, many a player does what's known as steaming. A *steaming* player doubles far earlier than normal for fear of missing her market and takes doubles that any sane person would drop. As a result, the steamer either makes a miraculous recovery or, more likely, watches her losses rise exponentially.

Figure 6-6 shows a classic steamer's error. Black uses the three principles to determine that she should double to 8 and White should quickly drop because he loses a gammon 45 per cent of the time. And yet, when I had this position, my opponent (a strong player) snapped up the 8-cube with but a second's thought!

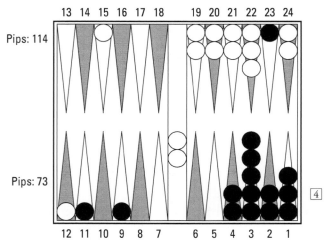

Figure 6-6: A steamer's take.

To understand why he took this double, I need to take you back one move. Prior to my last roll, White was winning the game and quite possibly a gammon, but then I rolled 22 and played bar/23*, 6/4(2)*, 3/1 (this move is better than 11/9 because it keeps Black's attackers diversified). White rolled 43 and stayed on the bar.

The change of fortune took my opponent by surprise and he struggled to come to terms with how a single roll transformed the game.

My next roll was 53, hitting a third checker with 23/15*, and I won a gammon and 16 points. Beware of steaming!

Freezing

Freezing is the opposite of steaming (see preceding section): a player well ahead on the score plays to protect her lead to make sure that she ends up winning for the evening. As a result, a freezing player drops doubles she ought to take and doubles far later in the game than she should.

A freezing player often ends up winning lots of single points instead of doubles because she offers a double when her opponent is way beyond the point of being able to take it.

Playing the opponent

You must play the opponent as well as the board. If you can get a read on your opponent and his cube habits, you can refine your own doubling to maximise your winning chances.

As an example, years ago I played an unknown opponent in a tournament. In matches, testing your opponent early on is always a good idea. After about five rolls each in the first game, I gave what I considered an early double. To my surprise, he dropped. In the next game, encouraged by this behaviour, I doubled even earlier. He dropped again! This pattern went on for six games (6–0 to me) before he finally came to life, but by then it was too late.

Too often I've heard someone say, 'I didn't double him because I thought he might take.' If you play with fear, you never become a great player. The vast majority of early game doubles are also perfectly correct takes, so try to leave emotion out of it.

Doubling decisions should not be influenced by the value of the cube. If you drop a double to 4 but would have taken the same double to 2, you're playing for too high a stake.

Redoubling Quandary: When Is Your Position Too Good?

The final variation on doubling I cover is what to do when you've taken a double and have turned the game round in your favour to the extent that you're a huge favourite.

Should you redouble and take two points? Well, sometimes that's the correct play, but quite often you may do better by playing on for a gammon and four points.

In Figure 6-7, a logical White would drop a redouble to 4 like a shot. Instead of offering a redouble, as Black you need to play on, attack the blot on your 3-point and try to blitz your opponent off the board. You may have to take your two points by redoubling later on when your gammon chances have diminished, but for now just play on.

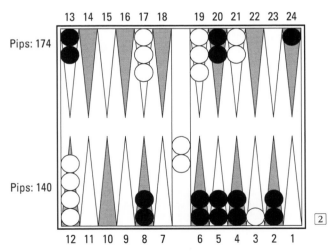

Figure 6-7: Deciding not to redouble.

Chapter 7

Planning Tactics for the Middle Game

* *

In This Chapter

▶ Planning your middle game

▶ Demonstrating basic middle game tactics

* *

*T*he opening phase of a game of backgammon can last a couple of moves or a couple of dozen moves. A whole game can be over in just two moves, in which case the opening is brief indeed!

But this chapter is concerned with the middle game. And, what normally happens is that after a flurry of hits or quiet manoeuvring, the game settles down into one of a number of easily recognisable patterns.

In this respect, backgammon is quite different from chess. In chess, memorising by rote huge numbers of opening sequences is possible and games can follow paths often trodden before, so that even after 15 moves you're still in 'the opening'. In the 1970s, many chess masters got bored with having to memorise so many opening sequences so they switched to backgammon, where they could analyse from first principles, contribute to theory, and get far more enjoyment from their playing.

The middle game is the most complex part of backgammon and developing a good grasp of how to play it takes time. So, don't worry if at first the middle game seems difficult. After all, if you could master backgammon in a week, it wouldn't be one of the greatest games of all time. (I'm slightly biased, but I believe it to be *the* greatest game of all time!)

In the middle game, the pattern recognition skills I talk about in Chapter 1 become paramount. If you can recognise that you've seen a similar position to the one in front of you, then with a bit of luck you'll have some idea of what to do. Alternatively, if the board looks completely new to you, you may well have trouble in deciding on a plan.

Having a Plan

Make sure that you always have a plan! Whether building a house, crossing the Sahara on a camel, or simply enjoying a few games of backgammon, things work so much better if you've an idea of what you're trying to do. In any backgammon position, you always need to have in your mind what you're trying to achieve.

Your backgammon plan needs to consist of a broad strategy determined by your position. In a certain position, escaping the last back checker may be the critical element of the plan; in another, building a prime in front of your opponent's two back checkers might be the key to success. The important thing is to identify your key objectives and then work towards them.

Prioritisation is key when planning. Many plans are multi-faceted because you may have more than one objective in a given position. In that case, you need to prioritise your objectives so that you try to achieve the most important ones first.

Backgammon is a dice game and so of course the dice may wreck your plan. Adopt flexibility and a willingness to adapt your plan depending upon what the dice dictate. A plan can cover the next few rolls or the next fifty rolls (rare!) – it all depends upon the position.

Figure 7-1 shows a typical middle game position. Black still has two checkers trapped in White's home board while White has only one checker back. Black has two objectives:

 ✔ Move his back checkers out of White's home board

 ✔ Prevent White's last checker from escaping Black's home board

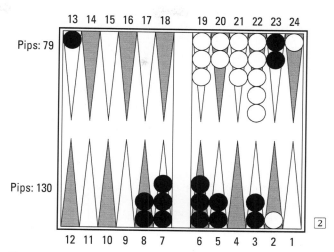

Figure 7-1: Making a plan.

And now comes the tricky bit. In backgammon you're subject to the vagaries of the dice and so while you might have a plan, the dice may not cooperate.

When the dice behave, everything is easy, and with a roll of 32 Black can play 7/4, 6/4 and complete a six-point prime, trapping White's single checker behind it. With double 5s or 6s, Black can move his two rear checkers to safety. The problems come when you don't roll perfect numbers.

A *perfecta* is what it sounds like – the perfect roll that enables you to achieve a critical objective. A particularly lucky roll is known as a *joker*, and an unlucky roll is known as an *anti-joker*. A perfecta is slightly better than a joker! A perfecta normally ensures that you win the game – a joker helps you considerably but it won't necessarily be decisive.

Taking any backgammon position, deciding on your basic game plan, and then working out how you'd play all possible 36 rolls is a good way to improve your game. Some of the 36 rolls may force you to change your plan!

Demonstrating Basic Middle Game Tactics

Some basic middle game tactics are tried and proven, and in these sections I give you examples of the most common ones to help you with your own decision-making process.

Backgammon is a dice-based game, so getting the dice to work in your favour is a good idea. I don't mean by cheating (!) but by making sure, as far as possible, that you can usefully use the majority of the 36 dice rolls. (The Cheat Sheet at the front of the book has a dice table that shows these 36 possibilities.)

Diversifying your good numbers

Diversification is the principle of playing in such a way that as many numbers on the dice as possible play well for you on your next turn.

Figure 7-2 shows a simple application of the principle of diversification.

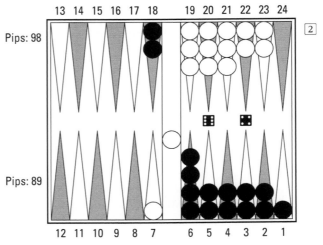

Figure 7-2: Diversifying your numbers.

Black has a strong position and a simple game plan. He wants to cover his blot on his ace-point and to hit White's blot on his bar-point. With his roll of 64, Black is forced to play 18/12 – this move is the only legal 6. Notice that if he leaves the blot on his 12-point, he needs 5s on his next turn, both to cover his own ace-point blot safely (6/1) and to hit White's blot (12/7*).

Needing the same number next turn to do two things isn't, however, a good idea. So Black should play 12/8 with the 4. Now he needs a 5 to cover his own blot and a 1 to hit White's blot. The number of dice rolls that do something good for him next turn significantly increases.

Duplicating your opponent's good numbers

If diversifying your own numbers is a good idea, then it follows that duplicating your opponent's numbers must also be a good idea.

The principle of duplication is to give your opponent lots of things to do with the same number so she's faced with a difficult choice.

Duplication can occur as soon as the second move of the game, as Figure 7-3 shows.

White opened with 21 and played the normal 13/11, 6/5. (Chapter 4 explains opening moves.) Black responds with a roll of 63. Black has many ways to play the roll but his best move is 24/15.

Now White needs either a 1 or 3 to hit Black's blot on her 10-point but she also needs a 1 or 3 to cover her blot and make her 5-point.

Giving your opponent difficult decisions to make is one of the routes to winning backgammon. After all, if you give someone the chance to make mistakes, they undoubtedly take that chance occasionally!

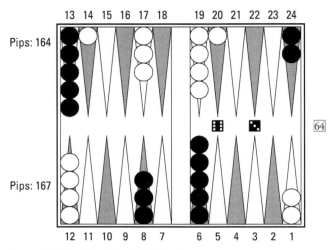

Figure 7-3: Applying basic duplication.

Picking and passing

In the opening rolls of the game, you can quite happily hit an opponent's blot in your home board and leave your own blot exposed because the risk is worthwhile to build new points. As the game progresses and you and your opponent both build up the strength of your home boards, leaving blots lying around ceases to be a good idea as a hit can prove fatal.

Using a technique known as 'picking and passing' can introduce a modicum of caution. *Picking* is to hit a blot in your home board and *passing* is to then move the checker used to make the hit to safety.

In the situation he faces in Figure 7-4, Black's plan is to get his last two checkers home and then bear them off. Getting those last two checkers home is easier if White is on the bar. He can play safely by moving 6/1 but the better move is 8/4* (picking) and 4/3 (passing), which gets one of those two last checkers home and leaves White only three rolls she can use – 53, 35, and 44 – to get in from the bar and then hit the blot on Black's 8-point.

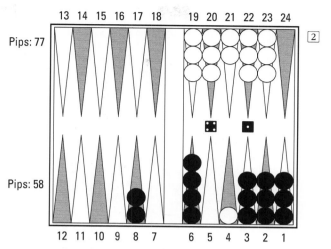

Figure 7-4: Picking and passing.

Priming and attacking

When the game starts you and your opponent both have two back checkers. As games evolve you sometimes find situations where your opponent hasn't managed to escape either of her checkers. Alternatively, in other games she gets one back checker as far as her mid-point or beyond and leaves one still in your home board. Handling these two situations is fundamentally different.

One of backgammon's most useful sayings is: 'Prime an anchor, attack a blot.' In other words, when your opponent still has two checkers back (an anchor in your home board), try to build a prime in front of them. If she has only one back checker, then attack it for all you're worth.

A little thought shows why this principle works so well: to escape one checker from behind a prime may be just possible, but to escape two or more is much more difficult. Conversely, if your opponent has only one checker back she can never create the safety of an anchor in your home board, so attacking the blot becomes an attractive game plan and prevents it escaping.

Although these ideas form the right general approach, they must be tempered by whatever is happening on the rest of the board.

In Figure 7-5, assume that you have 22 to play, as Black.

Small doubles are nearly always difficult to play because they provide you with so many options – just one more reason why having a plan is so important. Playing to a plan helps you to focus your ideas.

Notice that White's back checkers are still in the start position, so building a prime to try to keep them there is a good plan. After using your first 2 to play the forced bar/23 to get your checker in, play the rest of the roll 6/4(2), 13/11. Doing so gives you four good points in your home and outer boards, and if you can then make your 5-point, you have a five-point prime that will probably be good enough to enable you to win the game.

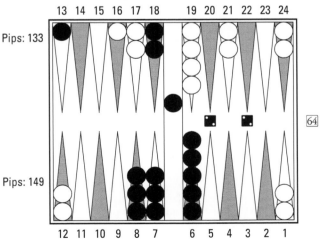

Figure 7-5: Priming an anchor.

On the flip side, look at the position in Figure 7-6, and decide how you play 42 as Black.

Your opponent has only one checker back and has a five-point prime on her side of the board. You can try to build a prime in front of White's checker and play 15/9 with that intent. However, if you obey the 'prime an anchor, attack a blot' principle, you hit the White blot in your home board with 5/1* and use the 2 to move 8/6. 8/6 is better than 15/13 because your priority next turn, assuming that White stays on the bar, is to cover the blot on your 1-point and you need to bring checkers within direct covering range of the 1-point.

This play may seem unduly risky but consider:

✔ Your home board is strong and White may not be able to get in and may stay on the bar.

✔ The tempo you gain may be critical in escaping your own rearmost checker.

✔ If left to her own devices, White may well attack your rear checker – after all, you've only got one checker back as well!

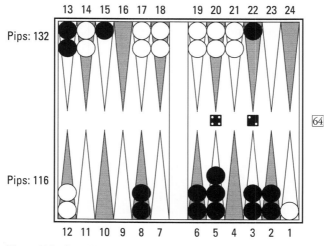

Figure 7-6: Attacking the lone rear checker.

Backgammon is all about the balance between risk and reward and acquiring the knowledge to make accurate judgements takes time. You may think that leaving a blot in your own board in this position is completely unwarranted but after you understand the demands of the position, it becomes mandatory.

Many players just make moves without ever considering their overall plan. If you can consistently play with a plan in mind you quickly become better than your opponents.

Paying now or paying later

The final tactic is one that occurs time and time again and is known as 'Pay me now or pay me later'. The principle is to decide whether to take a risk now to increase your winning chances or postpone it until later because the risks are actually too high.

As Black in the position shown in Figure 7-7, your plan is to bring those last two checkers on your 10-point into your home board – preferably without leaving White a shot at a blot. You can play your roll of 43 in two ways:

- 6/2, 6/3, leaving no blots and hoping for a miracle roll next turn.

- 10/6, 10/7, leaving White a shot if she rolls a 2. If White gets a 2 and hits your blot, she's likely to win the game, but if she misses you probably won't give her any more opportunities.

The problem with 6/2, 6/3 is that unless you roll doubles other than 55 next turn you'll probably have to leave a blot (or blots) anyway. Leaving the minimum number of blots this turn (and while White still has a blot in her home board) in exchange for future safety is thus better.

This problem is relatively straightforward but be warned: 'Pay me now or pay me later' problems can get much more difficult!

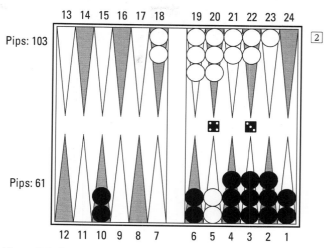

Figure 7-7: Pay me now or pay me later?

Chapter 8

Discovering Strategies

*T*he majority of backgammon middle games fall into a number of clearly defined categories, and to become a good player you need to know the correct strategies for each type of game and how to apply them. In this chapter I discuss the various types of games and strategies for playing each.

Racing toward the Finish

Unless an early double offer is dropped, in every game of backgammon a time comes when the two sides disengage from each other and charge forward in the race to bear off checkers. Sometimes one player is well ahead of the other and the winner is a foregone conclusion (though you can never take anything for granted in backgammon!).

Winning races is all about optimising the play of the dice to make the best use of the numbers that you roll, so that you can get your checkers into your home board as quickly as possible and then bear them off as efficiently as possible.

Many races are very close, and in these situations, knowing the pip counts becomes vital so that you can make the right decisions about doubling. (I explain pip counts in Chapter 5.)

BACKGAMMON LORE

Hoping for middling dice

Lewis Deyong, long-time MC at the World Championships at Monte Carlo, used to say three kinds of dice existed:

✔ Great dice that help you win no matter what your opponent does.

✔ Bad dice where the converse is true – you lose, no matter what.

✔ Middling dice, which were key for him. He expected his skill would let him win more games than his opponent because he knew what he was doing!

Bearing into your home board

You can't take any checkers off until all 15 are in your home board so the priority must be to get all your checkers home as quickly as possible.

You don't need a lot of skill to position your checkers in your home board as you bear them in, but even so I offer a couple of guidelines to follow so that you create what is known as an efficient bear-off:

✔ Try to get as many crossovers as you can with each roll. A *crossover* occurs when you move a checker from one quadrant of the board to the next.

✔ Try to ensure that you get at least some checkers on each point but put the majority of your checkers on your 6-point, 5-point, and 4-point. The reason for this action is purely arithmetical. If you put too many checkers on the lower points, you 'waste' pips on the dice bearing them off later on (for example, using a 6 to bear off a checker from your 1-point). Positions where most of the checkers are on the high points minimise wastage.

An old backgammon saying states that you can never have too many checkers on your 4-point and the artificially created position in Figure 8-1 demonstrates the importance of this point.

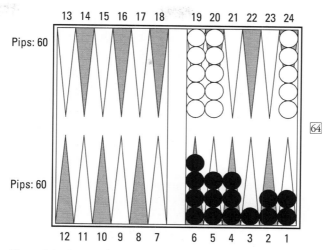

Figure 8-1: An awkward bear-off.

Black has a nice smooth position, with the majority of her checkers on the high points. Whatever number she rolls, she takes checkers off. Not so White, who won't bear off checkers with rolls of 4, 3, and 2 and wastes time and rolls moving checkers to fill the gaps.

Worst of all, at the end White 'wastes' pips. He's rolling 4s, 5s, and 6s and taking checkers off his 1-point. As an example, every time he rolls a 6, he 'wastes' 5 pips.

You may think this doesn't matter but it means that he probably made inefficient use of his numbers earlier. He may well require an extra roll to bear off his checkers than he would have done with optimal play.

An extra roll may mean losing a game rather than winning it so bearing off efficiently is important.

Holding Position in Anchor Games

An *anchor game* is one in which you hold an advanced point in your opponent's board, normally his 5-point or 4-point. Holding such an anchor is a tremendous advantage because:

> ✔ You always have a place to re-enter a blot if you get hit.
>
> ✔ You can't be blitzed (I explain later in the section 'Braving a Blitzing Game').
>
> ✔ You can't be primed.

In this section I look at when and how to utilise the anchor and, importantly, when to give it up and make a run for home.

In general, the higher the point you hold in your opponent's home board, the better off you are.

The lower down your opponent's board your anchor is, the more you have to rely on hitting and the less likely that you can win the race. Also, if you're way back on your opponent's 2-point or 1-point, sometimes you just can't get those checkers moving. You may find that your opponent has borne all his checkers off before you get the rear checkers home and thereby lose a gammon. Losing a gammon isn't a good idea, so take care!

Understanding how to handle the doubling cube in these situations is also critical. I cover all these points in the next sections that look at the various anchor games.

In all the examples of anchor games in the following sections, I show the standard positions, and although the game plans I outline remain fundamentally the same, your doubling decisions can be influenced by differences in the positions. For example, if you have three or even four checkers back, your position is much worse and you lose more gammons. Conversely, your opponent's board may not be as perfect as those I show and in that case your winning chances are better.

Playing holding games

Other than races, the easiest type of games to play are holding games. A *holding game* is one in which a player has an anchor on her opponent's bar-point, 5-point, or 4-point. If the opponent has a similar anchor, you're in a *mutual holding game*. I examine both types in the next sections.

Holding on the 5-point

Figure 8-2 shows a typical 5-point holding game.

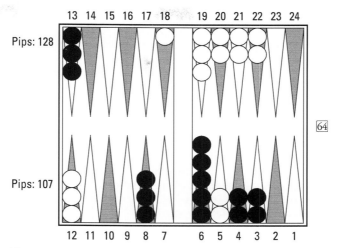

Figure 8-2: A typical 5-point holding game.

Black has escaped both rear checkers as far as her mid-point. Meanwhile White has taken possession of Black's 5-point and has started to build a strong home board. The game plans are relatively straightforward:

- **Black's** strategy is to bring her checkers home without leaving White a shot at hitting her. Ideally, she wants to roll a big double to clear her mid-point safely.

- **White** can win the game in one of two ways:

  - Catch up in the race and then win it. If a big double puts him ahead in the race then he should abandon the anchor and head for home. As for Black, a big double would come in useful.

  - Wait for Black to leave a blot and then hit it. The strength of his home board should then guarantee the win.

The doubling cube is obviously important and knowing when to double and when to take is crucial. The rule of thumb here is that you can double when you have a 20 per cent lead in the race, and your opponent can take the double even when he has a 50 per cent deficit in the race. How can that be? Remember that White can win in two ways, racing and hitting. As his racing chances diminish, his hitting chances increase and these balance out so White can nearly always take your double!

This doubling advice applies to the situation in Figure 8-2. If Black has checkers on an extra point in her outer board, particularly her bar-point, then things change significantly and the doubling decisions are much more akin to those in a pure race. This change is because Black is much less likely to leave a shot as she brings her checkers home.

One of the beauties and/or frustrations of backgammon is that a small change in a position can result in different doubling decisions. But then, would you want to play the game if everything was straightforward?

Playing a mutual holding game

Figure 8-3 shows both sides with advanced anchors. Black has escaped as far as her opponent's bar-point – a common situation. And White has taken up residence on Black's 5-point.

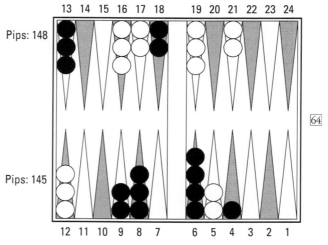

Figure 8-3: The mutual holding game.

Not surprisingly both players have similar game plans, which have three elements:

- ✔ Roll a big double and run for home. Players don't need to feel disgraced in planning for a big double. After all every sixth roll, on average, is a double.

- ✔ Build new points, preferably in front of your opponent's anchor, without leaving unnecessary blots in order to do so.

- ✔ Build new home board points. The stronger your home board becomes, the more you limit your opponent's ability to make risky plays. He won't voluntarily leave blots if you have five points in your home board.

Normally one player or the other rolls a double and the game evolves into a 5-point or bar-point holding game. Only then do you need to think about doubling, and I explain this issue in the preceding section.

Anchoring on the 4-point

Figure 8-4 shows a typical 4-point anchor game, which is similar to the 5-point game. As Black, your plan is to patiently build your home board using the checkers on your 8-point and mid-point and wait for a shot. Hitting the shot normally entails you giving up your anchor but that's fine as that was the plan in the first place! Occasionally you'll catch up in the race but most of the time when you win, you win because you hit a shot.

Because you're not on White's 5-point, he can play certain numbers fairly easily. For example, if White rolls 52 he should play 13/8, 13/11, clearing his mid-point and leaving you just a 7 to hit the blot. If you miss, he probably won't have much trouble bearing in safely.

Until White clears his mid-point, you can take a double even with a large deficit in the race. But once the mid-point is cleared, base your decision purely on the race.

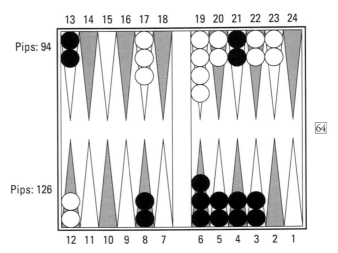

Figure 8-4: Waiting on the 4-point.

Trying an anchor on the 3-point

Black's anchor is back one more point, on White's 3-point, in Figure 8-5.

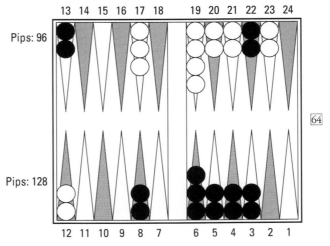

Figure 8-5: Holding the 3-point.

Despite being worse off than you are with an anchor on White's 4-point, this situation is still an easy take if you're doubled.

Your game plan remains the same as with a 4-point anchor – build a strong home board and wait for a shot. Because you're further back, you get more shots but you win the race less frequently than you do with a 4-point anchor. For example, rolling 55 doesn't help much because you can't escape your back checkers, which are blocked.

The 3-point game is remarkably resilient, and an old backgammon adage says 'A 3-point holding game is always a take'. Surprisingly, most of the time this saying is true.

Avoiding the smaller anchors

When you find yourself on your opponent's 2-point or 1-point late in the game, suddenly things take a turn for the worse.

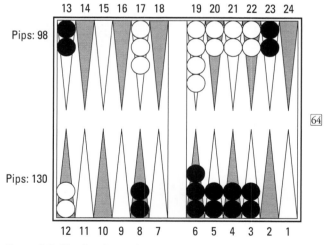

Figure 8-6: The 2-point anchor game.

From the position Black holds in Figure 8-6, she still gets a lot of shots, but sadly also starts to lose a fair number of gammons.

If you're offered a double from this position, drop. If you've already been doubled by the time you reach a position like this and you own the doubling cube, your game plan remains to build your home board and wait patiently for a shot. Sometimes you may abandon the anchor, at least with one checker, in order to start to run off the gammon but try to hold it for as long as you can.

The 1-point (or ace-point) game is the worst of all. Now you virtually never win the race and must rely on hitting a shot but from the 1-point you start to lose a significant number of gammons so, if doubled, you must drop like a shot.

Braving a Blitzing Game

A *blitz* is exactly what it says – an attempt to wipe your opponent off the board with a violent attack in which you show scant regard for your own safety.

For a blitz, the basic strategy is to hit and keep hitting and to bring fresh attackers, normally from your mid-point, to the scene of the battle in your home board as quickly as you can. Don't worry too much about your back checkers. They can stroll home later after you've won the war!

Of course, sometimes your blitz fails and your opponent gains an anchor in your home board. Recognise this reversal of fortune and switch game plans.

When blitzes work, they quite often lead to gammon wins but when they fail they can leave your opponent with the advantage. Such is life – you can't win them all!

Blitzing early

Whenever your opponent doesn't have an anchor in your home board, you always have the potential for a blitz. Normally blitzes are initiated by rolling a double and pointing on one (or more) of your opponent's checkers. This has the dual benefits of improving your home board and sending your opponent to the bar. If he fails to anchor quickly then you can continue to aggressively attack, or blitz, him.

Rolling an early 55 after your opponent has split her rear checkers, as shown in Figure 8-7, presents the most common opportunity for an early blitz.

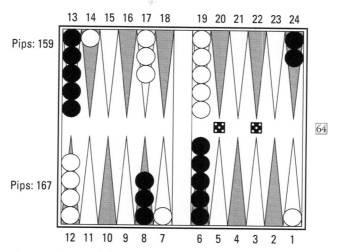

Pips: 159

Pips: 167

Figure 8-7: An early blitz.

White played his opening 62 by moving 24/18, 13/11. Black now rolls 55. The correct blitzing play is to make two home board points and put White on the bar with 8/3(2), 6/1(2)*. Doing so gives Black an immediate three-point home board and a powerful threat.

In fact, if White rolls one of the nine rolls that prevent him from getting his checker in, the game's over! Black should double and White should drop the double. This situation is the shortest possible game of backgammon.

But let's assume White enters with 42 and plays bar/21, 13/11. Black then rolls 62. To keep the blitz going, Black needs to keep hitting by moving 13/7*, 6/4* and putting two checkers on the bar.

The idea of a blitz is to never let your opponent anchor and just keep pounding away at his blots.

Black's strong home board will come in to play at some point, and as soon as White fails to come in from the bar, Black probably has a powerful double.

Blitzing in the middle game

The majority of blitzes happen in the early game, normally when you roll a good double and your opponent is caught napping. But, blitzes can happen at any time.

The difference is that by the middle-game both players have usually made new home board points. This gives the blitzer an advantage because he has points ready-made but the defender also benefits because when she hits a shot from the bar her home board is stronger and may help to slow down the blitz.

However, the criterion for a blitz remains the same. If your opponent has no anchor and one or more vulnerable blots, then this position always has good blitz potential.

In Figure 8-8, Black has her opponent on the bar and a four-point home board. If you're Black, plan to blitz White. With any 3 or 4, you hit White's blot on your 4-point and can then try to fill in your 4-point and 5-point and close him out.

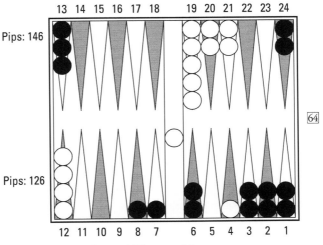

Figure 8-8: Executing a middle game blitz.

A *close-out* is when you own all six points in your home board and your opponent has one or more checkers on the bar.

Don't be put off by your opponent's good home board or the fact that your rear checkers haven't yet started on their journey home. If your blitz fails you're likely to lose, but if it succeeds you usually have time to escape those back checkers, and you may well win a gammon.

Forget half measures here. With a roll of 31 you can play 7/4*/3, picking and passing, but to complete your blitz you need to get ownership of your 4-point so you must play the bolder 7/4*, 24/23. It may look dangerous to leave a blot in your home board but when you play a blitz you must commit to it wholeheartedly.

Backgammon champion Paul Magriel once said that to play winning backgammon 'you must put 'em where you want 'em' – very good advice.

In this position you want the 4-point, so do your utmost to make it!

Going Prime Versus Prime

Prime versus prime and back games are the two most complex types of middle game in backgammon, and you need to play many games of each type before you become comfortable with them.

A *prime versus prime game* is one in which both players have a prime of at least four points and have one or more of their opponent's checkers trapped behind it. Figure 8-9 shows a basic prime versus prime position.

Both players have five-point primes and both have two checkers trapped behind their opponent's prime. The only difference is that Black has an anchor on White's 3-point while White's back checkers are split.

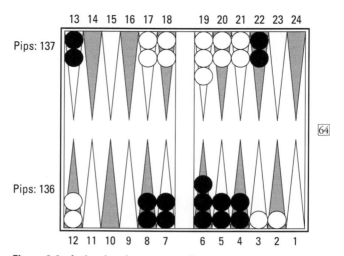

Figure 8-9: A classic prime versus prime.

Sorting out a strategy

The three basic elements for playing prime versus prime positions are:

- ✔ Get to the edge of your opponent's prime.
- ✔ Leap the prime.
- ✔ Knock your opponent away from the edge of your prime.

Remember these three rules and you won't go far wrong. The problem comes in prioritising them when you've a choice of more than one of them.

As Black in Figure 8-9, with a 32 roll, if you follow the rules, you play 6/3* (hitting from the edge of the prime), 13/11 (nothing better!). The key is to avoid plays such as 8/6, 8/5, which weaken your prime.

Reducing your prime is nearly always wrong unless doing so helps you to adopt an even better game plan.

Never forget that backgammon is a dice game. If the dice dictate a change of game plan, go with it. Sticking obstinately with the wrong plan keeps your opponent happy and you out of pocket!

As an example of changing your plan to suit your roll, in this position if you roll 54 your best play is 8/3*, 7/3, switching to a blitzing attack.

Moving with zugzwang!

In chess, the term *zugzwang* refers to the compulsion to move and is used when a player has to weaken his position by moving. Zugzwang can happen in prime versus prime positions and Figure 8-10 shows a classic example.

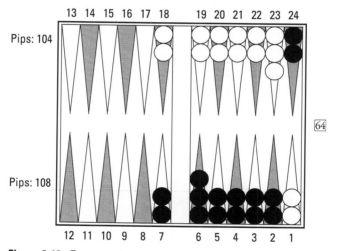

Figure 8-10: Zugzwang!

Both sides have full primes restraining their opponent's rear checkers. Whoever has to give up her full prime first is at a disadvantage as her opponent may then be able to escape.

If you're Black in this position, you can play rolls of 11, 12, and 13 without breaking your prime, but your best roll is 66 when you can't move at all! This roll forces White to surrender his prime first unless he rolls 66 in return.

One last thing to consider in prime versus prime positions is the number of checkers trapped behind the primes. The more men you've trapped the better, as more checkers imprisoned significantly reduces your opponent's options. Conversely, if you have more than two checkers trapped, beware the doubling cube – lots of prime versus prime positions end in gammons for the winning side.

Playing Back Games with Anchors

Back games happen when you get a lot of blots hit early in a game and you end up making two or more anchors in your opponent's home board. Figure 8-11 shows a typical back game.

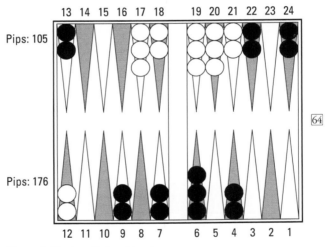

Figure 8-11: A well-timed back game.

As Black you own White's 1-point and 3-point. Back games are known by the anchors you hold, so this is a 1–3 back game. If you owned White's 1-point and 2-point, it would be a 1-2 game, and so on.

Notice that you're way behind in the race – a 105 to 176 pip count – so to win the game you have to hit a shot and then contain the blot you hit by restraining it behind a prime.

Your basic strategy for playing a back game is as follows:

- ✔ Establish two anchors in your opponent's board.

- ✔ If you have more than four checkers back, try to escape the extra checkers.

- ✔ Build a strong home board, preferably making the points in order (6-point, then 5-point, then 4-point, and so on) to give yourself a prime to contain any checker you hit.

- ✔ Hit a shot and then contain the hit blot.

This strategy may sound straightforward but believe me it isn't and back games are fraught with danger. A couple of big doubles, for example, can completely destroy your plans and lead to positions like the one Black faces in Figure 8-12.

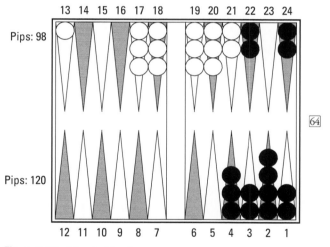

Figure 8-12: A busted back game.

Now even if you get a shot and hit White's blot, you can't contain it. As Black, you virtually never win from this sort of position.

Avoid back games if you can. When you lose, you often lose a gammon.

In the early 2000s, the London backgammon scene was graced by a player known as 'Back Game Billy'. He'd try to play a back game at every opportunity. He compounded this flawed strategy by not playing his back games particularly well technically. As a result, his bank balance took heavy hits!

Each back game has its own characteristics, but if you're forced into playing one then the best are the 2-3 and the 1-3. The 1-2 is also good provided you have the timing to play it, that is, the ability to keep your strong home board while waiting for a shot.

Follow these guidelines if your opponent is the one who's playing the back game:

- ✔ Try to keep your checkers in front of your opponent's anchors and try to build a solid prime in front of them.

   Don't be afraid to leave blots to achieve this situation. Having a checker hit early in the development of a back game rarely hurts, as your opponent's home board is likely to be weak at this point.

- ✔ Try not to stack too many checkers on one point as you bear in. Flexibility is the key word.

Part III

Bearing Off (The Last Lap)

The 5th Wave   By Rich Tennant

'Doubling the cube is known as a "beaver," or a "raccoon." What you're doing is known as a "chicken," or a "dodo," or a "donkey," or a...'

In this part . . .

Part III looks at how to bear the checkers off the board – the final stage in any game of backgammon. I give you lots of tips on how to stay ahead right until the end.

Chapter 9

Bearing Off without Contact

• •

In This Chapter

▶ Rolling out the end-game

▶ Adding up with Robertie's method

▶ Deciding doubles by numbers

• •

*U*sing pip counts and the other rules I explain in Part II to determine when to offer and take doubles are all very well when you still have quite a long way to go in the race, but when you get down to the last few rolls of the game you need more accuracy.

Certain positions occur so often that you just have to become familiar with them. The play of the checkers is normally trivial, but the key is how you handle the doubling cube. Endings can be volatile and the cube can bounce around like a bull in a china shop. Make sure that you can pay if you lose.

In this chapter I aim to help you stay in the winning column with tips on when to double and when to take. This chapter deals with the most common positions that come up time and time again. Positions that require more complex treatment I'll leave for another day!

Assessing No-miss Positions

In positions in which both sides have an equal number of checkers, the player whose turn it is has a tremendous advantage. If nobody rolls a double, the player who goes first wins the game. However, a double occurs once every six rolls on average, so the trailing side has some chance to roll a double and win the game.

When the checkers are stacked on the lower points in the home boards, you end up with what are called *no-miss positions*. These are positions where each player takes off (at least) two checkers on every turn no matter what he rolls.

Because no-miss positions come up time and time again, knowing the correct doubling cube actions for them is vital.

In this section I go through no-miss positions that take from two to five rolls (without doubles) to end a game. Black is the next roller in each scenario.

In Figure 9-1, each side has four checkers. Would you double as Black? Would you take as White? I hope your answers are yes and no.

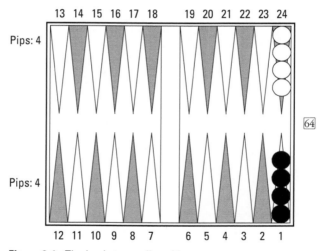

Figure 9-1: The basic two-roll position.

Black wins immediately if he rolls a double, and even if he doesn't, White needs to roll an immediate double herself.

To calculate White's chances of winning, you multiply the chances that Black doesn't roll a double by the chances that White does. The dice table on the Cheat Sheet at the front of the book shows 6/36 chances of rolling a double, so Black has 5/6 chances of not rolling one, and White has 1/6 chances of rolling one, which gives White 5/36 chances of winning or 13.9 per cent. That position's a long way from the 25 per cent White needs in order to take.

Giving each side two more checkers means that each player needs three rolls (excluding doubles) to bear off, as is the case in Figure 9-2.

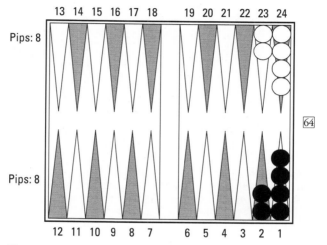

Figure 9-2: The basic three-roll position.

If Black offers a double, does three rolls give White enough chance to roll that all-important double?

Her position's close but the answer is no. White wins just over 21 per cent of the time – still 4 per cent shy of the magic 25 per cent. I haven't shown the arithmetic because you can just memorise the percentages from this book – much simpler than doing the maths!

In Figure 9-3, each side is going to be off in four rolls at most. Of course, Black still doubles, but now White has enough time to roll a double and her winning chances are up to about 27 per cent, so she can take.

Any roll that isn't a double – all 30 of them – are known as *non-doubles*.

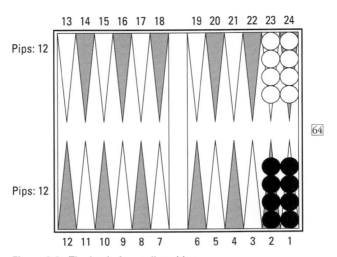

Figure 9-3: The basic four-roll position.

A key point is that, by accepting the double, White gets value from owning the cube. After the sequence: non-double from Black, double by White, and another non-double from Black, White reaches the position shown in Figure 9.1 with her on roll. Black has to drop White's redouble from this position.

In a 5-roll versus 5-roll position, Black is correct to offer a double and White has a comfortable take.

Interestingly, if you already own the cube in a 5-roll versus 5-roll position, don't redouble until you have a 4-roll versus 4-roll position.

Using Robertie's Addition Method

One of the problems (or is that attractions?) of backgammon is that really small changes in a position can lead to very different plays and cube actions.

Bill Robertie, the American Master and one of only three players to win the Monte Carlo Backgammon World Championship twice, coined the term *Addition Method* for his way of evaluating these positions. Robertie's method works best when only a few checkers are left on the board, typically less than seven on each side.

Robertie's Addition Method is actually simple: you add up all the ways that you can win the game and if that figure comes to greater than 25 per cent, you can take a double.

You can use this method for more complex middle game situations but obviously in those situations you have to do a fair amount of estimating of your winning chances rather than using exact percentages.

When using Robertie's Addition Method in the endings, the most useful things to remember are:

- ✔ The chance that the losing side can pull out a win in a 2-roll versus 2-roll ending is approximately 14 per cent.

- ✔ The winning chance for the losing side in a 3-roll versus 3-roll ending is approximately 21 per cent.

- ✔ The chance of rolling any specific non-double is 5.5 per cent.

- ✔ The chance of rolling any specific double is 2.75 per cent.

- ✔ The chance of rolling a specific number from 1 to 6 (excluding doubles) two rolls in succession is approximately 8 per cent.

- ✔ The chance of rolling a specific number from 1 to 6 (excluding doubles) three rolls in succession is approximately 2 per cent.

Armed with this information, you can do far better than your opponents when it comes to close decisions. Nothing's better than accepting the cube in a losing position and then winning the game! Your opponent, unless she's made of stern stuff indeed, may let the loss affect her for the next several games.

Black is doubling in Figure 9-4, which is a 3-roll versus 3-roll position. Can White squeeze out a take?

Noticing that Black can't take a checker off with a 32-roll is the key here. That roll happens exactly once in 18 rolls, which translates to 5.5 per cent.

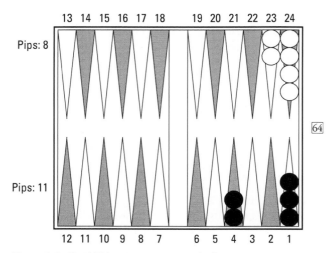

Figure 9-4: Can White squeeze out a take?

The preceding list tells you that a 3-roll versus 3-roll position gives the losing player a 21 per cent chance to win. Using Robertie's addition, you add 5.5 per cent to 21 per cent to get 26.5 per cent – enough to take!

Counting on the 8-9-12 Formula

In *pure* races, that is, when there's no contact between the two armies, you can use the *8-9-12 racing formula*. You can use the formula for any race longer than 30 pips – there's no upper limit.

> ✔ Double if you've an 8 per cent lead in the race.
>
> ✔ Redouble if you've a 9 per cent lead in the race.
>
> ✔ Accept a double if you trail by no more than 12 per cent.

In Figure 9-5, Black leads by 5 pips (about 11 per cent of 46) so he should definitely double. White trails by less than 12 per cent so she should take (12 per cent of 46 is about 5.5).

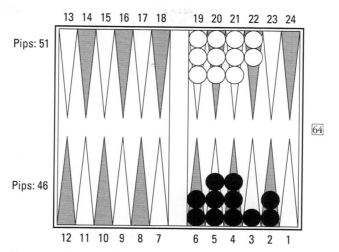

Figure 9-5: Black leads by 11 per cent so should definitely double.

For most positions with what I call *normal distribution*, that is, no huge stacks of checkers on any one point, you can use the 8-9-12 formula and get it right most of the time. Once the pip counts get below 30, you sometimes need to consider the number of rolls left for each player and Robertie's Addition Method may come into play as well. As ever, the more you play the more familiar you become with handling these endings.

Chapter 10

Bearing Off Against Contact

In This Chapter

▶ Taking men off when your opponent's trying to get in

▶ Moving off against an anchor

▶ Bearing off against two anchors

*O*ften when you start to bear off your checkers, you're still in contact with your opponent. Your opponent either has a checker on the bar or an anchor somewhere in your board.

Now, instead of just taking off checkers, you have to take far more care. Nothing's more galling than having one of your opponent's checkers on the bar unable to get in, then leaving a blot, having it hit, and ultimately losing the game. Of course, nothing's more satisfying than reversing that scenario and winning by hitting a late shot!

Bearing Off when Your Opponent is on the Bar

Most of the time when you have at least two men on every point in your home board so that your opponent is closed out and he can't get a checker off the bar, you win the game. But sometimes the dice just don't cooperate and despite your best intentions, you leave a blot, get hit, and lose the game.

In this section I look at how to optimise your winning chances when you've closed out your opponent's checker.

Getting them home

In this section I help you make sure that you leave shots as infrequently as possible by showing you how to position your checkers in the best possible places as you bear them into your home board.

Your work to expose no blots and protect your win begins as soon as you close out your home board. You need to keep potential future rolls in mind and set up your board to give yourself options.

Going in high

When you bring those last few checkers home, the idea is to put the spares on the high home board points – points 4, 5, and 6 – as shown in Figure 10-1.

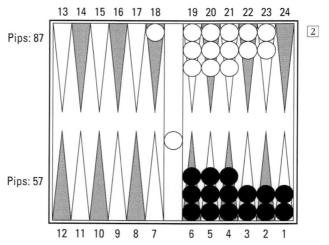

Figure 10-1: Establishing the optimal bear-off position.

This structure gives you the most flexibility and you're unlucky if you have to open a blot and leave a shot from here.

Considering 66

A rule of thumb says that if you can play 66 safely, you can play any roll safely. So consider your next roll before you make your current moves.

Figure 10-2 shows Black with just her last three checkers to bear in.

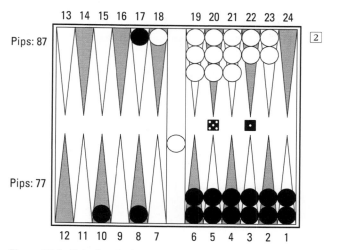

Figure 10-2: Bringing the last checkers home.

As Black, you can play 51 with no apparent danger. Not much difference seems to exist between moving 17/12, 8/7 and moving 17/11. But consider how you can play 66 next turn:

✔ If you move 17/12, 8/7 with the 51, you play 66 next turn by moving 12/6, 10/4, 7/1, 6/off. Your home board is still closed off and you're completely safe.

✔ After 17/11, you have to play a 66 roll by moving 11/5, 10/4, 8/2, 6/off, leaving White a potentially game-winning shot from the bar.

Granted, the above are small differences, but over time small differences add up so taking care to get things right is worth it.

Getting them off

When you've got all your checkers home, follow these rules for bearing off:

> ✔ Try to keep an even number of checkers on your highest occupied point.
>
> ✔ Try to keep an even number of checkers on your two highest occupied points.
>
> ✔ Clear from the rear – that is, bear off checkers from the 6-point and then the 5-point, and so on.
>
> ✔ Try to avoid leaving gaps.

If you follow these rules, you leave blots far less often than if you play without plan or purpose.

Figure 10-3 shows the sort of position that you really don't want to end up with. You've an odd number of checkers on your 6-point and an odd number of checkers (5) on your two highest points. You're forced to leave a blot next turn if you get any roll with a 6 (other than 61) or 55. That's ten numbers – way too many!

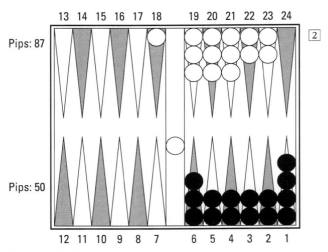

Figure 10-3: An unattractive bear-off.

If you follow my guidelines for bearing off, you'll win most of the time, which is just what you want, and if your opponent has lots of his own checkers to bear in, you'll win a lot of gammons too.

Staying Afloat with an Anchor in Your Home Board

In this section I explain the tactics you can apply when your opponent holds an anchor in your home board.

Of course, how serious a threat the anchor poses depends upon which anchor your opponent holds. If he's on your 5-point and you've got all your checkers in your home board, any chance of losing the game disappears after you clear your 6-point. However, if he holds your 1-point, he's a threat until the end of the game.

The further back in your board that your opponent holds an anchor, the more games you lose. The good news is that the further back that the anchor is, the more gammons you win.

The rules I establish in the preceding 'Getting them off' section for playing against checkers on the bar largely hold true for most anchor games as well. I don't have the space to cover the few exceptions, and as they're very few, those basic rules will serve you well for the vast majority of your games.

Notice incidentally that the side with the anchor wins only if it can contain a hit checker. If all your opponent's checkers other than the anchor are piled on the 1-, 2-, and 3-points, a hit can often save him a gammon but rarely enables him to win the game.

Navigating the ace-point game

If your opponent holds your ace point, the odds are that he'll get a shot 90 per cent of the time. Of course, he still has to hit the shot and win the game, but 90 per cent is a high figure so be prepared.

Figure 10-4 shows a well-timed ace-point game. From this position as Black, you win about 80 per cent of the time. That's a good percentage but it means that you lose 20 per cent of the games. Losing from what is apparently a winning position is upsetting but that's the beauty of backgammon – just when you think you're home free, disaster strikes out of a clear blue sky and it can strike quickly.

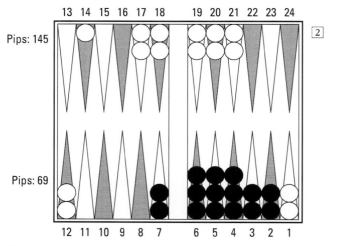

Figure 10-4: A well-timed ace-point game.

If you roll 65, for example, you must play 7/2, exposing a blot on your bar-point. Now if White rolls a 6, you're in dire trouble and virtually lost.

You can't do anything about such sequences. Just accept that they happen and that you'll lose from time to time. On the other side, you win a fair share of games when you're the one sitting on an ace-point.

Deciding whether to stay or go

When you're the one holding the anchor, you often have to make the choice between staying for a last-ditch shot or running away to try to save the gammon.

The choice can be complex and a number of factors come into play:

- ✔ How likely are you to save the gammon?
- ✔ How likely is it that your opponent is going to leave a shot next time?
- ✔ How likely is it that you may hit an exposed blot?
- ✔ If you hit a shot, can you contain the hit blot?

You've no magic formula to balance all of these factors. You need playing experience and reference positions before you start to make the correct decision most of the time.

Here's a good example that covers many of the preceding points. In Figure 10-5, if you throw any roll with a 6, your decision is made for you – you have to run the last checker as doing so is the only way to legally play a 6. But what about 54?

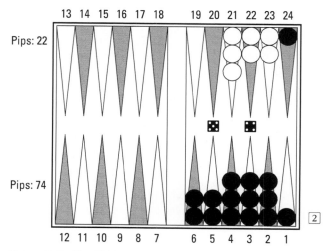

Figure 10-5: Should I stay or should I go?

You can play 6/1, 6/2 and hope that White exposes a blot next turn (he does so on 32 of his 36 possible rolls!). The trouble is, you then have to hit the shot and then win from there. You have twin problems – White already has 10 checkers off and you've lost your 6-point.

Sadly, you just don't win often enough to make the risk of staying worthwhile. You're better off just running away with 24/15 and (hopefully) saving the gammon. Sometimes discretion is the better part of valour.

In backgammon, you have times when you just have to accept that you're going to lose. You cannot win every game you play – far from it. Successful backgammon is all about maximising your winnings and minimising your losses.

Doubling the Weight with Two Anchors

If your opponent has a *back game* – two or more anchors in your home board – bearing in is much more difficult because you can't play some numbers as you'd like – which is the purpose of a back game after all!

The basic rules still apply: you try to put spare checkers on the higher points in your home board, consider what rolling a 6 would mean to you, and clear from the rear.

Killing numbers

When playing against back games, a few techniques are worth knowing. The first is known as *killing numbers*, which means that certain numbers can't be played legally.

By killing your big numbers, you give your opponent more time to weaken his home board so that, if and when he does hit a shot, he's no longer able to contain the hit checker.

In Figure 10-6, White would like to get and hit a shot while his home board is still strong but unfortunately for him, he may have to weaken that board next turn. Meanwhile, you have to play 32.

Playing 10/5 and giving yourself a smooth distribution on your higher points may look right, but a better move is 10/8, 9/6, because if you roll a 6 next turn you won't have to play it as you have no legal plays. As you still have a six-point prime,

White can't move his back anchors next turn and needs to weaken his home board to some degree – unless he gets double 6s and can't move either.

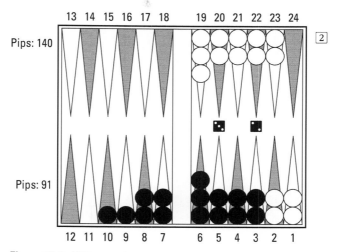

Figure 10-6: Killing numbers.

Checking your numbers

As well as killing numbers (see preceding section), my other piece of advice about back games is to think about specific numbers. The number (or numbers) you think about are different for any given position but the bigger numbers tend to be the more awkward. For example, if I make this move this turn, how do any of my 5s play next turn?

Each back game has its own peculiarities. In Figure 10-7, White is playing a 1–3 back game, and the game is reaching its climax.

A peculiarity of the 1–3 back game is that you have difficulty with 3s and 5s. You can't move 6/3 or 4/1 or 3/off, so all your 3s have to be played from your 5-point. So put extra checkers on your 5-point when you're bearing in.

In Figure 10-7, Black has piled her 5-point high, but just to show how perverse the game can be, imagine that your next roll as Black is 33. You have to play 5/2(4), leaving White a double shot – whoops!

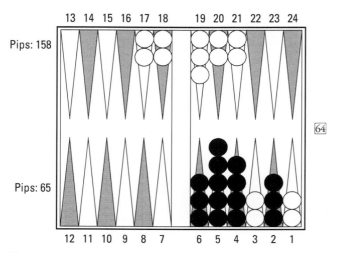

Figure 10-7: Looking good but . . .

Knowing when to double a back game is a useful piece of information. You consider many factors, including the strength of your opponent's home board and his ability to hold onto his two anchors, but assuming he has a strong home board and can keep his anchors, the general rule is as follows: double your opponent when you have three more points to clear in front of his most advanced anchor.

Referring to Figure 10-7, Black has a perfect double and White has a strong enough position to risk taking.

Part IV
Varying the Play

'My strategy is to use a Pinot Grigio opening, a Chardonnay running game, and finish with a Grand Brut bear off.'

In this part . . .

Backgammon has many fun varieties of play, including chouette, tournament play, and playing online. You'll never be bored playing backgammon, but if you fancy experimenting with the game, this part will give you plenty of options.

Chapter 11

Looking at Complex Endings

*M*any backgammon games end with a simple race to bear-off the checkers but if that happened all the time life would be dull indeed. Many interesting things can happen in the ending and wild swings of fortune are possible late on, generating lots of excitement.

In this chapter I look at some of the possible endings.

Winning after Hitting a Late Shot

So, your back-game strategy (explained in Chapter 10) pays off and you hit a shot late in the game, probably from a deep anchor. What happens next?

A number of key factors influence your next moves and whether you're likely to win the game or not. The factors are:

✔ **How many checkers your opponent has borne off.** This is the most critical element. If your opponent has already borne off 14 checkers, then you have a different goal to when she's only borne off 2 or 3. In the first case, you're trying to save a gammon; in the second, you've realistic chances of winning.

If you manage to close out the hit checker, you become favourite to win if your opponent has borne off 7 checkers or less. With 8 checkers off, you're virtually 50/50 to win the game.

✔ **The strength of your home board.** If you have a closed home board, you're far better off than if all your checkers are piled on your 1-point and 2-point (in which case you can hardly ever contain a hit checker).

✔ **The position of your checkers.** Hopefully, your checkers are in good positions to build/extend a prime and/or hit your opponent's checker as it tries to scamper around the board.

✔ **The position of your opponent's remaining checkers.** This is the converse of your own situation – does your opponent have a good home board and active checkers?

✔ **The doubling cube.** Normally, if you own the cube, you can use it to win the game at the appropriate moment (or at least give your opponent a difficult drop/take decision). Without access to the cube you must win by checker play alone.

Your late-hit strategy is relatively straightforward: you trap your opponent's checker behind a full (six-point) prime; roll your checkers home; and win the race or win with the doubling cube.

Clear as mud? Time then to bring a little clarity to matters and look at the various aspects of this strategy, which I do in the next sections.

Building a prime

Building a full, six-point prime and keeping it as long as you can, ensures that your opponent cannot escape because she cannot leap the prime.

The simple rule for building a prime is *slot and cover*, meaning slot on the first roll and cover on the second. *Slotting* means putting a blot on the point you want to make next and *covering* means adding a second checker to secure the point. You can slot the front or the back of a prime. Normal play is to slot the back but occasionally you have to slot the front and expose a blot to a direct shot.

In Figure 11-1, as Black, you hit a blot on your opponent's 5-point and she isn't able to re-enter on her next roll.

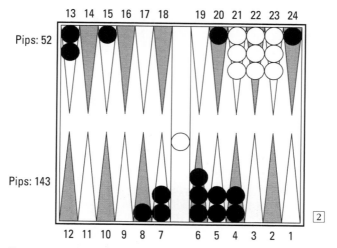

Figure 11-1: Hitting a blot on your opponent's 5-point.

You've already a four-point prime from your bar-point to your 3-point, and you have a checker on your 8-point.

Your first task is to extend your prime to six points. With any 5, 7, 12, or 16 on your next roll you can make your 8-point and have a five-point prime. (Note that with a roll of 53, your best choice actually is to make your 3-point with 8/3, 6/3, building a five-point prime and a stronger home board.) To complete your prime, you then need to make your 3-point or your 9-point. As your opponent is still on the bar, you may find it easier to make the 9-point. In Figure 11-2, the game has moved forward a couple of rolls: White has re-entered, and you have your five-point prime and are looking to make your 9-point for a full prime.

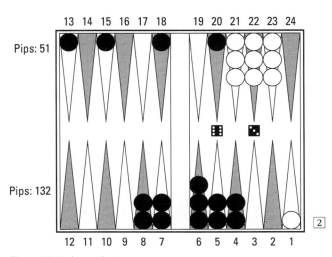

Figure 11-2: Later that same game. . .

If you're very lucky, you roll 64, play 15/9, 13/9, and have your six-point prime immediately. In backgammon, though, you can't be lucky all the time; you have to make your own luck. What if you roll 63? The answer is 18/9, slotting the back of the prime (18/9 leaves two direct numbers to cover the slot next time so this move is better than any other play). Unless White rolls 26 and hits the blot, you're a big favourite to be able to cover it and complete your full prime on your next turn.

You want to make your opponent's escape as difficult as possible so, in addition to the slot and cover rule that I discuss earlier in this chapter, add one more: if your opponent gets to the edge of your prime, hit her away from the edge if you can do so without weakening your prime.

In Figure 11-3, White's blot is on your 3-point poised to escape with a 6 next time. You have the same roll of 63 as in the previous example. Obeying both rules, the correct play is 15/9, 6/3*. This play slots the back of the prime and hits the opponent away from the front of it. Now White needs to get to your 3-point and roll a 6 to escape – if she rolls 36, you know it's just not your day!

If you roll 65, you could play 15/9, 8/3* but doing so weakens your prime by reducing its length and thus breaks one of the rules. In this instance, playing 20/14, 18/13 is better. If White doesn't roll a 6 next time, you can hope to attack the blot or make your 9-point. If she does roll a 6, then only 66 and 65 are really good for her. With any other 6, you have a double shot at her to send her back behind your prime again.

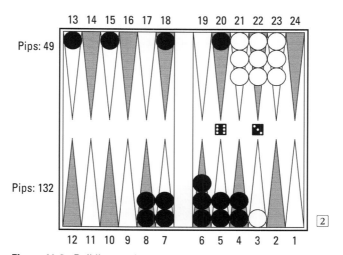

Figure 11-3: Building a prime under direct threat.

Note that 18/9 is the wrong idea in this situation because, if White does roll a 6, she not only escapes but also puts your checker on the bar, severely reducing your chances of hitting back next turn.

This change of strategy is driven by the tactics of the position. Having a flexible strategy is one of the keys to playing successful backgammon.

Rolling home a prime

All being well, you make your full prime and keep your opponent trapped in your home board. Now, you need to *roll the prime home*, which means moving the prime into your home board until you end up with a closed home board and your opponent's checker on the bar.

The technique you use to roll a prime home is quite simple – you use the old slot and cover that I discuss in the preceding section. You slot the next point in the prime with one roll,

then cover it next time. The difference is that this time you
slot the front of the prime with impunity – if your opponent
hits the blot, you just bring the prime around until it's once
more ready to join the fray. This strategy is zero-risk as your
opponent can never escape from behind a full prime.

To demonstrate, assume that you roll 52 in the position shown
in Figure 11-4. As Black, you're at the stage where you've built
your full prime and your opponent is on your ace-point.

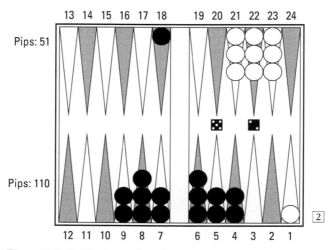

Figure 11-4: Rolling home the prime.

You slot the next point you want to make (your 3-point) by
playing 8/3 and using the 2 to move 18/16. You could play the
2 6/4 – the two plays are similar – but bringing the further-
most checker closer to home is the normal tactic.

You hope that you can make the 3-point next turn. Then you
can start work on your 2-point, and so on, until eventually you
reach the position shown in Figure 11-5 – a closed-out home
board.

Most of the time the dice co-operate and you're able to
achieve a closeout. However, rolling a prime home can take
quite a while and as the old idiom says, 'there's many a slip
'twixt cup and lip'. A big double, particularly 44, can often dis-
rupt your plans and force you to break your full prime.

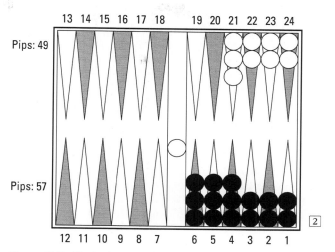

Figure 11-5: Black closes out White.

Occasionally your opponent escapes despite your best efforts and you lose the game – such is backgammon. All you can do is play to the best of your ability and generally the prime rolls home smoothly.

Bearing off to victory

So you achieve your target of closing out the hit checker. You now enter the final stage, which is bearing off to victory.

If the doubling cube is on your opponent's side of the board, you have to win by bearing off your checkers more quickly than your opponent. Hopefully, when you finally open a point in your home board, your opponent stays on the bar long enough for you to win the game comfortably. (Chapter 10 lays out strategies to use when your opponent is on the bar while you're bearing off.)

However, if you had checkers in your opponent's home board while she was bearing off, you've probably been doubled and so own the cube. You can use the cube to good effect either to win the game by doubling your opponent out or by giving her a difficult take/drop decision. The question is: when do you redouble?

Today, computers help with exact calculations, but even before computers lent a hand, US master Bill Robertie came up with a useful rule of thumb: redouble when you've borne off five fewer checkers than your opponent. At that point, your opponent has a borderline take/drop decision to make.

Robertie's rule extends to cover a situation in which you close out two of your opponent's checkers. Then you can redouble when you've borne off ten fewer checkers than your opponent.

The situation in Figure 11-5 in the preceding section exactly meets Robertie's rule. Black has borne off no checkers and White has borne off five. Therefore, Black should double. The more difficult decision belongs to White.

And, what if you're the one who's hit late in the game? If your opponent has the optimal bear-off structure of a closed-out home board and her three spare checkers on the high points, you can double if you've borne off 11 checkers or more. White has a take if you've borne off exactly 11 checkers; otherwise she must drop.

A number of factors to take into account can affect Robertie's basic rule. I talk about each in the next sections.

Considering your home board

Obviously, if you have open points in your board, your opponent can enter more easily, and the more open points you have, the weaker your position is.

Placing your spare checkers

You use 12 of your checkers to build a closed-out home board. Put the remaining three on your 6-point, 5-point, and 4-point. If you can't do that, keep them on the higher points if at all possible (the dice don't always cooperate).

Figure 11-6 shows a weak position in which all spare checkers are on the ace-point. As Black, you wouldn't yet be able to double.

Now, although your pip count is lower, your position isn't as strong as in Figure 11-5. On your next roll, you'll probably have to open one of your points, giving your opponent a chance to enter much earlier than she would do from the earlier position. This relatively small change turns the position from a double into no double. You must improve your position a little before doubling.

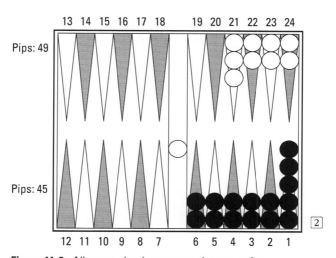

Pips: 49

Pips: 45

Figure 11-6: All spare checkers are on the ace-point.

Contemplating your opponent's checkers

Robertie's rule works most accurately when your opponent won't miss when her hit checker returns to its home board – that is, when all her checkers are on her lower points.

In Figure 11-5 in the previous section, although White has checkers on all her lower points, if she rolls lots of 1s, 2s, or 3s, eventually she'll fail to take a checker off, which may prove fatal for her.

In that position, you have the optimal bear-off position and she has a home board weakness. This position means that she has to drop your redouble.

Figure 11-7 shows a position that often arises when you've been playing with an anchor on your opponent's 1-point and hit a late shot. White's having no checkers on her 1-point makes a huge difference because she won't be able to bear off when she rolls 1s and she must drop a redouble. Taking would be a blunder.

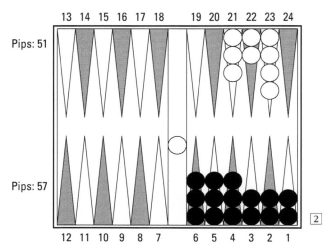

Figure 11-7: Spotting an opponent's weakness.

Backgammon is a game of small differences and just moving a checker one pip, particularly in the ending, can make a huge difference. Make use of reference data but always remember to allow for the actual position you see in front of you.

Becoming Aggressive under Duress

What happens when your opponent is favourite, even after you make a late hit and have a closed-out home board?

If your opponent has borne off eight checkers before being hit and closed out, then she's a slight favourite. As the number of checkers off increases, the more of a favourite she becomes until, with 14 checkers off, she's 93 per cent likely to win the game.

But, backgammon is about risk taking, and when your opponent is well ahead you have to take a few risks to win the game.

Figure 11-8 shows a classic example of a situation that calls for aggressive play. If your only concern is safety, you play 6/1, 6/4 with a 52 roll. However, you've borne off two checkers while White has taken off ten. To catch up, you need to take risks. Your choices are 6/4, 5/off or 5/off, 2/off.

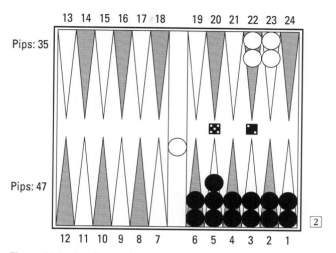

Figure 11-8: Bearing off aggressively.

The 5/off, 2/off play is better for three reasons:

- ✔ It takes off two checkers instead of one.

- ✔ White doesn't get 66 as an immediate winning roll.

- ✔ If White enters from the bar with rolls of 22, 23, or 24, she'll still be stuck in your home board. Even worse, if she rolls 21 she has to play bar/23*, 3/2, giving you a new blot to shoot at.

  Just when you thought you were losing, real winning chances appear apparently out of nowhere!

As you may have deduced by now, using the doubling cube to good effect is critical in these endings – used well, it can save you an awful lot of heartache.

Meeting the Coup Classique

One particular ending occurs often enough that I'll introduce you to it now so you know what to do when it occurs over the board. The ending is called the Coup Classique.

Setting the scene

Would you like to be Black in the position shown in Figure
11-9? No, and neither would I. If White rolls any doubles
other than double 1s, you lose a backgammon and hand
over six points. Backgammons may only happen once in a
hundred games but you'd much rather it was your opponent
who lost one!

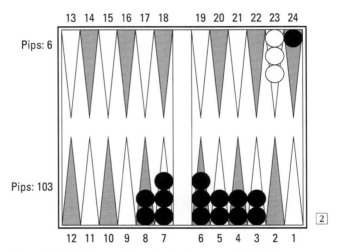

Figure 11-9: All the makings of a backgammon for White.

If White rolls any two different numbers without a 1, she bears
off two checkers and you've one last chance to save the
gammon by rolling a 1 next turn. If you hit that last checker,
you have a 7 per cent chance to win the game.

Now look what happens if White rolls any 1 other than double
1s. She has to play 2/off, 2/1*, leaving the position shown in
Figure 11-10.

Suddenly you have real winning chances! If you roll a 1 or 2,
you can certainly save the gammon, and if you can hit and
close out both of White's last two checkers, you become
favourite to win the game.

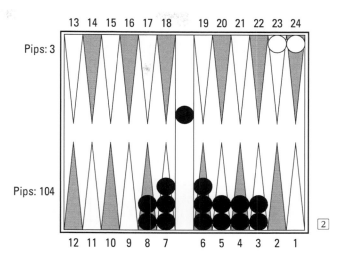

Figure 11-10: Black with a double shot.

Executing the coup

To maximise your chances of winning, you need a little bit of technique, which I explain here.

The easy case is when you hit with a 1. Leave that checker on your opponent's ace-point as long as possible with the hope that you roll another 1 to hit the second blot.

Your situation is a bit more difficult if you initially hit the checker on White's 2-point. In that scenario, you need to leave blots in your home board to get another checker sent back so that you can have another go at the other blot.

In Figure 11-11, if you (as Black) roll 64, don't roll your prime by making your 2-point with 8/2, 6/2. Instead, leave two blots by playing 7/1, 6/2! Now any 1 or 2 by White and you've a checker sent to the bar and another chance to pick up White's blot on her ace-point.

Assuming you manage to hit the second checker, then, and only then, do you blitz your opponent until you end up with a closed home board and her two checkers on the bar. (Refer to Chapter 8, which explains how to blitz.) All that remains is to bear off three checkers so that you've borne off ten fewer checkers than your opponent and offer your opponent the perfect redouble.

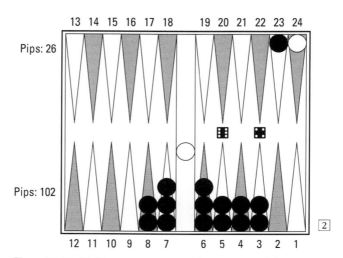

Figure 11-11: Making sure to expose blots – yes, really!

Executing a successful Coup Classique is one of the most satisfying moments in backgammon. Just like riding a bike for the first time, you feel a tremendous sense of accomplishment.

Conversely, losing to a coup takes all the wind out of you. Be careful not to over-react by taking doubles that you shouldn't in subsequent games in an attempt to regain the money you lost so unfairly in the coup!

Weighing Anchors

I explain how to play when your opponent has an anchor in your home board in Chapter 10. In this section, I look at the thorny question of when to abandon an anchor that you hold in your opponent's board and show you how to entice your opponent to abandon an anchor in your home board. You may have to make decisions on these issues in the middle game or in the end game.

Pulling out too soon

Taking up their anchor far too early is one of the most common mistakes made by beginners. And not only beginners make this type of error.

Figure 11-12 shows a position from the World Championship final of 1997. As Black, Frederic Banjout was playing Jerry Grandell and reached this position in a key game at the end of the match.

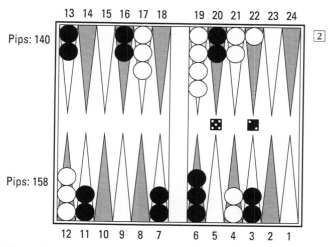

Figure 11-12: Championship position.

Had he simply played 16/11, 16/14, nothing bad could've happened to him. Instead he chose to abandon his anchor by playing 20/13. His punishment was swift and terrible to behold. Grandell rolled 33 and moved 13/10, 8/5(2)*, 6/3. Not long afterwards, he was chalking up a gammon and an unassailable lead in the match.

 What this example highlights is:

- ✔ Giving up an anchor early on is rarely right. The exception normally comes when you roll a big double and can run safely for home.

- ✔ Your anchor often protects you from losing a gammon because you can't be closed out if you hold an anchor in your opponent's home board.

- ✔ Your anchor provides long-term winning chances – those chances disappear only when your opponent clears all her points in front of your anchor, and even then you still have racing chances.

✔ When behind in the race, don't race is one of the most fundamental but simple rules for playing winning backgammon. Even if the race is really close, hanging on to your anchor is often right.

Banjout was behind in the race yet chose to leave his rearmost point, and subsequently lost the game.

In Figure 11-13, your natural temptation may be to head for the hills with this roll of 43 and play 20/13. Doing so puts you marginally ahead in the race and leaves you only one more checker to escape, so 20/13 looks tempting, doesn't it? The problem is that a single checker is always vulnerable to attack and this one is susceptible to a hit by any 1, 3, or 8. For example, if White's next roll is 32, she can play 8/5*/3 and gain valuable ground in the race. Even worse, you may stay on the bar.

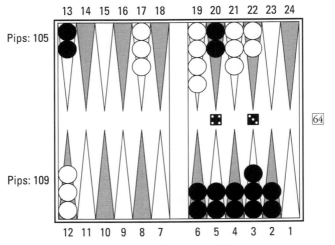

Figure 11-13: When not to abandon your anchor.

Sitting tight and waiting for a double so that you can move those rear checkers together in safety is the right plan here. Or you can sit tight and hope that White leaves you a blot to shoot at. The right move is 13/9, 13/10 – this gives you plenty of time to wait for something good to happen.

In Figure 11-14, the correct play isn't nearly so obvious but the same principles apply.

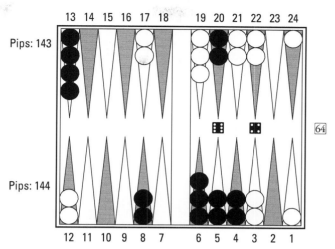

Figure 11-14: Keeping the anchor.

You can run away with 20/10 with a 64 roll – after all, what other move is there? The surprising answer is 13/7, 13/9! This may look dangerous at first sight but a few points help you realise that this move is the best one to make:

- ✔ You still have your anchor so nothing really bad can happen.

- ✔ If White doesn't hit, you have the chance to build a powerful prime in front of her back checkers.

- ✔ If she does hit you, she may have to give up her best asset – her 3-point anchor – to do so.

Finding plays like this isn't easy when you first start to play because they look risky, but actually they're just the opposite.

Trapping off an anchor

What can you do when your opponent has an anchor and you want her to go rather than stay? Can you get her to give up her anchor prematurely? Yes, you can with what is known as a *trap play*. This involves forcing your opponent off an anchor that she'd rather keep.

Figure 11-15 shows a classic opportunity for a trap. White's board is shot to pieces but she has the security of her anchor on your 3-point. Her strategy is to wait while you bring your checkers home and then hope to roll a double 6 at the right time to escape her checkers.

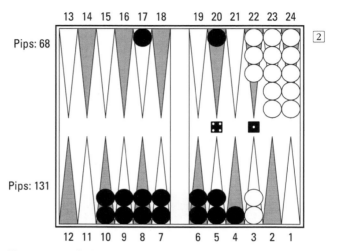

Figure 11-15: A classic opportunity for a trap.

You have to play a 41. The mindless play would be 17/12. Now look at the right play, 8/4, 8/7. When White next rolls a 5, she has to play it 22/17 and her anchor is broken – 51 and 52 are particularly bad for her. You can then attack the checker left behind and also hopefully recapture the one that escaped. All being well, you can close out both checkers and win a gammon.

You can normally execute a trap play only when your opponent's board is busted. If she has a strong home board, a trap is just too risky. Don't make a trap play until your opponent has all the checkers in her home board on three – or preferably two – points.

Like the Coup Classique described in the preceding section, trap plays are tremendously satisfying when they come off.

Chapter 12

Entering the Chouette

*A*fter the introduction of the doubling cube in the mid-1920s, backgammon took a huge leap forward in popularity, becoming *the* after-dinner entertainment at fashionable dinner parties. However, it was still a game for just two players. So, though many could proffer commentary and advice during a game, only two players were directly involved. In a world where gambling was all the rage, this situation seemed unfair to the spectators – though doubtless they bet on the outcome of games anyway.

And then in a stroke in the late 1920s, the two-person only problem was solved. Backgammon players adapted the version of the card game piquet in which a group of players compete against one other person, and used the same word to describe it – *chouette*.

Over the years the rules evolved considerably, but I describe those most commonly in play today.

I play most of my backgammon in chouettes. I love the cut and thrust of the discussion and the excitement of the big games. Time disappears when you play backgammon and even more so in chouette – many's the night I've played and seen the dawn break!

Listing the Reasons to Play in Chouettes

This version of the game is worth playing for a variety of reasons, some of them listed here. Playing chouette:

- ✔ **Provides a fast-track backgammon education.** Listening to good players consult about positions and how to play moves gives you a free education that may take you years to pick up in one-to-one play. Ideally, you play in a chouette with at least some players better than yourself. If you don't want to risk your money, just watch and listen to any high-level chouette – you can find out a huge amount just from being a spectator.

- ✔ **Exposes you to high-pressure situations.** Nobody becomes a good player without being able to handle pressure, whether financial or coping with a complex decision in a tournament final. Playing in a chouette, especially as the *box* (the person playing alone), gives you ample opportunities to handle pressure.

- ✔ **Improves your game much quicker than playing the same person week in, week out.** Playing with just one other person tends to reinforce bad habits. Playing with a group of people in a chouette quickly exposes those bad habits and prompts you to remove them!

- ✔ **Offers great fun.** Chouette is certainly the most sociable form of the game. And, after all, the social aspect is why many people play backgammon. The game's certainly not played in silence like chess! If a chouette is going on in the room, you certainly know about it.

Examining the Players and the Play

To understand a chouette, you need to be introduced to the cast of characters and understand the rules by which they play this wonderfully vibrant version of the game.

Introducing the players

A *chouette* is a French screech owl. In ornithology, the chouette is often set upon by other birds, and thus the term is ideal for the group game in which one person is pitted against a team of others.

Looking at the roles

In a chouette, each person has a different role to play:

- ✔ **The box:** The person who plays alone against the other players.

- ✔ **The captain:** Makes moves for the team, acting independently before team members can consult (see the next section). Even after team members have the right to add their suggestions, the captain still has the final decision about all moves in any case of argument – and believe me, arguments do happen!

- ✔ **The team or crew:** Players who are able to offer advice to the captain and can individually offer and take doubles.

At the start of a chouette, the various roles are decided by rolling the dice. The highest number gets the box, the next highest the captain, and the rest constitute the team.

Rotating players

The players rotate in strict order. Say Player A is the box playing against the team of B, C, and D, where B is the captain.

Player A	The Box
Player B	The Captain
Player C	Team Member
Player D	Team Member

If A wins the game she keeps the box, C becomes the captain, and B goes to the bottom of the queue.

Player A	The Box
Player C	The Captain
Player D	Team Member

Player B	Team Member

If the team beats the box, however, the captain, B, becomes the new box, C becomes the captain, and A goes to the bottom of the queue on the team.

Player B	The Box
Player C	The Captain
Player D	Team Member
Player A	Team Member

Partnering up with more than five players

Once the number of players gets beyond five, the box may well take a partner to spread the risk. Suppose A is in the box against B, C, D, and E and just as she loses the game F decides to join the chouette. His wish is easy to accommodate. B becomes the new box, A (the outgoing box) becomes B's partner, C becomes the new captain, and F just goes to the bottom of the team.

When the box has a partner, the same rules on consulting apply to them as to the team, that is, they cannot discuss moves until at least one doubling cube has been offered and accepted.

Theoretically, you can have as many players in a chouette as you like, but in practice I've found that seven is the maximum. When an eighth player arrives, creating two four-person chouettes is usual. Four or five is the optimum number, I feel. The game is relatively fast-paced and plenty of opportunities occur to get in the box — which is where the big money is won (and lost).

Explaining the play

The box always makes her decisions independently, but how the team opposing her determines which move to make depends on whether a double has been accepted.

In the initial plays, before a double, the captain decides on the moves on her own, which makes the game move right along.

A team member gains the ability to consult other team members about moves only after one of two things happens:

✔ The box takes the team member's double to 2.

✔ The team member takes the box's double to 2.

A team member who has doubled cannot consult with a team member who hasn't doubled and offer that combined advice to the captain.

Doubling in a chouette

As in all money games, the Jacoby Rule is always used in chouette play. Beavers and Raccoons are by agreement only and are almost never used (refer to Chapter 5 for more on these furry animals). What I describe in this section are the most commonly accepted chouette doubling rules but you're sure to find variations as you travel the backgammon world. Check on the local rules before you start to play with unknown opponents.

Each member of the team has her own doubling cube and makes her own cube decisions. Any one of the team can double whenever it's the team's turn to play.

Etiquette demands that all team members who want to double should make their intent clear and then and only then the box makes her decision. The team members don't need the captain's permission; they're free to act as individuals.

The box must offer an initial double to all the team members at the same time. Some team members may drop, in which case they lose 1 point. Others may take and they now play on for 2 points (or more if further cube action occurs).

If the box is redoubling, she can choose to only redouble some players and not others. Surely if she redoubles one, she should redouble them all? If she were playing against computers that would be true, but she's playing against humans and human beings make errors. A drop to some is a take to others and an astute box can maximise her winnings by using the doubling cube based on her knowledge of her opponents.

When the game ends, each player is debited or credited with the number of points she won or lost in the game and the box is credited (or debited) with her total winnings (or losses) from all the doubling cubes.

Developing Chouette Tactics

Much of the play in chouette resembles head-to-head play but subtle variations do exist and understanding how to vary your play to maximise your winning chances in this form of the game is important.

Accommodating weak players

In a chouette, you quickly discover the strength of the other players. If you play in a regular chouette, you know people's abilities before you start; if you're joining a new game, you quickly get a feel for who knows what they're talking about and who's just making up the numbers.

Weak players can survive in chouette by listening to their team members and taking advice. Occasionally, a weak player goes on a long winning streak just through good luck.

Weakness will out

A few years ago, a strong London chouette was graced by a man who just loved playing back games and would steer for them even when other game plans were better. In his first two months he won hundreds of pounds, decided he was a strong player, and refused all further advice.

But in backgammon, the luck evens out and in the next two months he lost thousands and hasn't been seen since.

When the box is a weak player, you expect to beat her, but what if your team captain is the weakest player? On every turn you fear that she's going to make a poor move and give the box the advantage. Doubling is the way to avoid this situation, simply to activate your ability to speak!

In Figure 12-1, as Black, your team has the edge, though a double would be premature in a normal game. (Note that when showing a position from a chouette, the done thing is to show all the doubling cubes.) However, if you're partnering with a weak player, you may well venture a double here so that you can advise your captain. Suppose her next roll is 42. On her own she may play 8/2. With you to help her, she plays 13/7*.

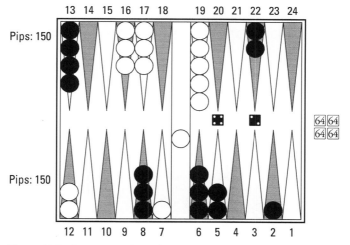

Figure 12-1: An opportunity to double to activate consulting privileges.

Playing in the box

In a chouette most players strive to get into the box, which is a strange ambition as the box is at a disadvantage. In one against many, the one sometimes misses a play or an idea, the many rarely do so.

In my youth I was lucky to have a series of lessons from Paul
Magriel, who has probably done more for the modern game
than any other person. His book *Backgammon* (Crown
Publishing Group) is still regarded as the bible of the game. He
gave me a crucial piece of advice on chouette play: '90 per
cent of the time your games in the box will define your
evening in terms of winning or losing. You're at a disadvantage, so make sure that you take a little extra time on each
play, even if only a few seconds, and for doubling decisions
always take more time than usual.'

When you're in the box, you play against a mix of styles and
personalities. You know you're playing well when you time
your doubles such that you get a split decision, that is, some
of the team members take and some drop. If all your opponents consistently snap up your doubles without a moment's
hesitation, you're probably doubling too early.

Figure 12-2 shows a complex position that's difficult to evaluate. Technically Black is not quite strong enough to double
but a sensible chouette tactic is to double. Some players see
the two exposed blots and drop while others note their 28-pip
lead in the race and 5-point home board and take.

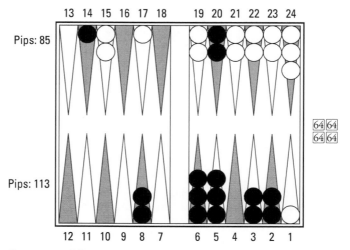

Figure 12-2: Offering a double to split the vote.

Giving your opponents the chance to make a mistake is the important thing. By offering them a difficult double, you do just that. Many players, as White, would drop this double, even though the double is a take.

Playing in the box can be stressful and you must accept that you'll have unlucky days, despite your best play. I played in the British Championships in the 1990s and was on the wrong side of very big cubes in a chouette that ran for the best part of four days – a very expensive weekend!

Ideally you treat every game on its merits but somehow people are always affected by their score. Figure 12-3 shows a position early in the last game of the night. White, the team, has just doubled. The conversation between the box and her partner, playing Black, went something like this:

> 'We're both well up on the night and, although I think that technically this is a take, I believe we should just drop this and call it a night. Losing a gammon in the box wouldn't be a good way to finish the evening.'

> 'I agree. Let's just drop.'

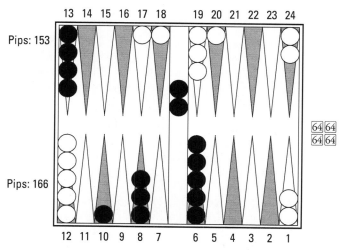

Figure 12-3: Dropping because of the score sheet instead of the situation.

And drop they did. Who knows what the result of that game may have been? They may have accepted the doubles and then won a redoubled gammon themselves. What I do know is that they didn't maximise their chances. When you drop doubles because of a fear of gammons or the lateness of the hour, you've lost the plot.

Guard against weak thinking and just play your natural game ignoring the points on your scorecard or the lateness of the hour.

Playing on the team

Playing in a chouette can be quite tiring, particularly if you have a long run in the box and have to concentrate for an extended period. When you're on the team, life can be a little more relaxing, unless you're the captain of course, when your full attention is required.

If you're just a team member, you can't do much during the opening moves of a game except hope that your captain finds the best plays. Use this time to get a breath of fresh air or a drink. Until you or the box turns the doubling cube, you can't offer your advice.

One golden nugget to keep in mind when you're on the team: you own your own doubling cube and have the right to make your own decisions. Don't be put off by what other players do – although it does make sense to study the actions of the better players.

Because each team member has her own cube, you may well see cubes end up on different values on different sides of the board in a chouette. This situation's part of what makes chouette play so exciting!

Assigning control of your cube when you step away

If you leave the area where the chouette is being played, you must leave your cube with someone; that is, you must designate someone to act for you if you're still away from the table when the cube's turned.

You normally select the strongest player in the chouette to act for you. The only exception is if that player is a big loser on the evening, in which case her cube actions may not be as rational as usual!

Nothing's worse than a team member who wanders off without leaving directions. When that situation occurs, normally the absent person's cube acts the same way as the captain's.

Bearing an unresponsive captain

Occasionally you encounter a captain who just won't listen to anyone. This type of player probably won't last long in the chouette, but in the meantime, just grinning and bearing the situation is the only option.

Curbing the arguments

By all means mention your ideas, but if not much difference exists between your play and the captain's, don't try to insist on your play at every turn – you rapidly become unpopular. Arguing about each and every play just prolongs the game and makes it less enjoyable.

Save your arguments for situations where it really matters. Figure 12-4 shows the power of a team in action in a high-stakes chouette.

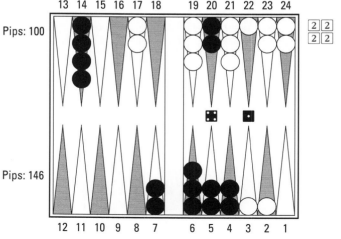

Figure 12-4: Arguing the play.

In this position the captain wanted to play 7/3*/2*, putting two of White's checkers on the bar. This play may look powerful, but isn't the right plan for this position. White has the better home board, so if your blot is hit on White's re-entry, you may well get stuck on the bar yourself. Also, White already has two checkers stuck behind your four-point prime. Extending the prime at the rear and trying to make your 8-point and 9-point is the right plan. Better moves are 14/10, 14/13, and 14/10, 6/5 (not exposing a second blot).

Although the captain was a weak player, luckily her partners were good players and quickly dissuaded her from her initial play. They briefly debated the merits of the other two plays, ultimately chose the best play, moved 14/10, 14/13, and went on to win the game.

Checking your Bank Balance before Joining a Chouette

In a chouette, the swings of fortune can be extreme so you need to make sure that you're comfortable with the stakes.

Playing as the box significantly increases the money you may be liable for. In a four-handed chouette, the box is playing against the other three players, and playing for three times the nominal stake. If the box wins, she gets a point from each player (assuming the cube hasn't been turned), but if she loses, she loses three points and three times the stake.

Everything is multiplied. If the box accepts a double from all three opponents in a four-player chouette, then loses a gammon, it costs her 12 points rather than the 4 points she'd lose if she were playing head-to-head. And 12 times the original stake can set you back a bit.

Losses in the box can be very expensive. One of the USA's top players recently claimed a world record by losing 300 points in a single game in a ten-handed chouette!

My rule of thumb for chouette is that you need to be sure that you can fund the loss of 200 points without it causing you a week's sleepless nights or a request for a bank loan.

Figure 12-5 shows a classic example of a situation in which money may easily influence play. The team own four cubes on 4. They now redouble you to 8. Do you accept?

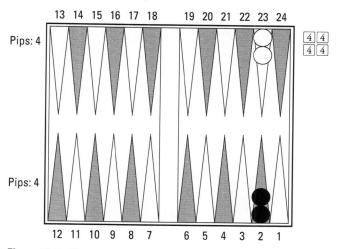

Figure 12-5: Money management.

In a head-to-head game with the cube still on 1, you'd take a double without a second thought because you know this position is a standard reference position and the correct cube actions are known to be double/take. But looking at losing 32 points – and 32 times the stake – may give you room to pause.

This choice is scary but accept the double. If the team rolls a 1 (except double 1s) you have a legitimate redouble to 16, which the team should accept.

So, if things go well you can win 64 points. But you can also lose 64 points. If you're playing for £10 a point, the potential swing on the next two rolls of the dice is £1,280 – quite a lot of money!

If you decide to drop the team's redouble to 8 because you may lose 32 or 64 points, you're letting the pressure of the situation get to you.

If you make doubling decisions based upon the value of the cube rather than on the position in front of you, you're playing for too much money.

Chapter 13

Playing Tournament Backgammon

. . . .

In This Chapter

▶ Looking at tournament play

▶ Doubling in tournament play

▶ Defining match play tactics

▶ Keeping the score in mind

. . . .

*T*he ultimate test of your backgammon skills comes when you venture into tournament play – the most difficult form of the game. Here, you have to use all your basic skills but also worry about the match score, too.

While many successful money players exist, the really great players are measured by their success in major tournaments.

Introducing Tournament Play

Tournaments can be one-day or one-week affairs with entry fees ranging from £5 to £1,000 depending upon the standard. You can choose a tournament that suits your pocket in the same way that you choose what level of money play you feel comfortable with.

Major tournaments have championship, intermediate, and beginner sections so you can have the fun of watching the experts and play at the same time. To find tournaments in your area, check out the Clubs and Tournaments section on the Chicago Point website at www.chicagopoint.com/links.html.

You can find a backgammon tournament every week of the year. Europe has a tournament circuit and the USA has another one. The two come together in the second week of July in Monte Carlo when the World Championships are played during a week-long tournament.

All you need to play in the World Championships is to have the entry fee and the wherewithal to stay in Monte Carlo for a week. The entry fee is currently about £750.

Most tournaments are just local club tournaments and quite often you don't even have to be a club member to play in them.

Paying to play

When you enter a tournament, you pay an entry fee and after that have no further financial obligation.

In big events, if you lose in the main tournament you automatically go into a Consolation tournament, which has shorter matches than the main event. If you lose in the Consolation, you go into the Last Chance, which is normally played with five-point matches.

In a really big tournament such as the World Championships you even get a Second Consolation before the Last Chance, so for the price of your entry fee you get to play in four tournaments.

Scoring the play

No, you don't have to write music while playing backgammon, but you do have to accumulate points if you want to advance in a tournament.

Nearly all backgammon matches are played to an odd number of points. If you play in a local tournament you probably play five-point or seven-point matches. If you get to the World Championship final, you play a 25-point match.

Playing with a clock

In the past, no time limit was placed on matches because in general backgammon is played at a reasonable pace. As players began to understand the complexities of match equity (see the upcoming section 'Playing to the Score with Match Equity Tables') and started doing calculations, the game slowed down and tournament schedules were thrown into disarray. Add to this situation the demands of television as the game became more popular and you can see that some form of clock became necessary.

Backgammon clocks are slightly different from chess clocks both in appearance and in how they work. In chess, you're allocated a set number of minutes for a specific number of moves. In backgammon, you start with a certain amount of time:

- **Time for the match:** You're generally allotted 3 minutes per the number of points the match is played to. So, in a seven-point match each player is given 21 minutes at the start of the match.

- **Time per play:** You normally get about 15 seconds to roll your dice and play your move before your time bank starts to count down.

The clocks (sometimes known as *Fischer clocks* after Bobby Fischer, the chess champion) manage both time elements. As soon as you've completed your play, you tap the clock, your timer stops, and your opponent's starts.

If you use up all your time before the end of the match, you lose the match, even if you're ahead in points.

Clocks add an exciting new dimension to match play. What was a difficult format is now even more challenging! Despite the complexity, playing with a clock is still my favourite version of the game.

Following the Rules about Doubling

One key difference between money and match play is that the Jacoby Rule, which states that you can't win a gammon if neither player has taken a double, is never used in match play. You can perfectly legally play on for a gammon with the cube unturned.

 Early in a long match doubling decisions are similar to money play but, as the end of the match approaches or if one player leads by a big margin, doubling decisions may be radically different from the norm.

The next sections talk about the various doubling rules that are in effect during match play.

Doing without doubling: The Crawford Rule

Introduced by one of the early backgammon giants, John Crawford, the *Crawford Rule* states that when one player reaches *match point*, which means they need just one more point to win the match, neither player can use the doubling cube in the next game. The game without the cube in play is known as the *Crawford Game*.

The player behind in the match (called the *trailer*) has no reason not to double after his opponent reaches match point. If he loses the game he loses the match anyway, so if he wins he wins two points instead of one and four points if he wins a gammon. The Crawford Rule guarantees that the leader doesn't have to face an immediate double based on nothing except the fact that he's ahead in the match.

 When you're the trailer, you *must* double at the first opportunity in all games after the Crawford Game. I've lost count of the number of times I've seen players forget to double!

Earning a free drop

In the first game after the Crawford Game, if the trailer needs an even number of points to win the match – for example, he's trailing 3–6 in a match to 7 – then the leader can drop one double without costing himself anything – he has a *free drop*. The trailer still has to win two games (excluding gammons) to win the match even after the leader drops a double.

If you're the leader, exercise your *free drop* at the first opportunity. If you lose the opening roll and your opponent moves first, then if your opponent offers an immediate double, that's normally sufficient reason to use the free drop.

If the trailer needs an odd number of points to win after the Crawford game, the leader must take all initial doubles. For example, if the score is 6–2 to 7 (trailer needs 5) then the trailer needs to win three games to win the match (assuming no gammons). If the leader drops a double, the score is 6–3 and the trailer now only needs to win two more games. You must make sure that you don't give him one of his three games for nothing so all initial doubles must be taken in this situation.

Making automatic redoubles

If the leader doubles when within two points of the match, the trailer has an automatic redouble. The reasoning behind this rule is that if the trailer loses the game, he loses the match anyway so he risks nothing when he loses but gains considerably when he wins, as he wins two extra points. You may think this tactic is an obvious one but time and again I have seen players forget to redouble.

Obviously this scenario is repeated where the leader is four points away from winning, holds the cube on 2 and redoubles to 4. Here the trailer has an automatic redouble to 8, so the leader must be even more wary of giving the cube away.

Strategising Match Play Tactics

Agreeing to play a match with the first person to score five points being the winner may seem fairly simple. And, in the early days of backgammon there probably wasn't much difference between money and match play.

However, as time went on, the good players began to develop match strategies and understand the influence that the score can have on checker plays and particularly on doubling decisions. In this section, I talk about those differences.

Getting to know your opponent

Unlike your normal head-to-head play or your regular chouette, in a tournament you play people you've never met before, so you've no idea of their playing strength and vice versa.

You need to try to get a handle on their skills as soon as possible. A bit like poker, getting a read on someone so that you can predict what they're likely to do in certain situations is really useful.

Applying pressure early by aggressive use of the doubling cube is the key to finding out what kind of player you're facing. To win a backgammon tournament, you always need luck but you need more skill in this form of the game than any other and knowing how to pressurise your opponent is fundamental to winning.

The most famous game in tournament history serves as a fitting example of pressure play. In the first game of a 17-point match, Walter Cooke, playing Black, doubled Jesse Sammis from the position shown in Figure 13-1. Many players pass a double when they're playing a back game in matches because of the fear of losing a gammon but Sammis was made of stern stuff and he correctly took.

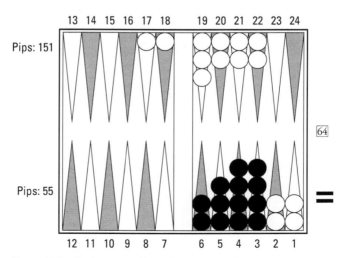

Figure 13-1: Cooke versus Sammis: pressure play.

Cooke rolled 65, played 6/off, 5/off, and Sammis promptly redoubled to 4. When Sammis missed both chances to hit the blot on Cooke's 6-point (known as a *double shot*), Cooke really put the pressure on by redoubling to 8, which Sammis took. When Sammis got another double shot later in the game, he redoubled to 16! This time he hit, and the game was in the balance for a while, but on the last roll Sammis needed to roll 66 to win. Recognising that being 16–0 down in a match to 17 was hopeless, he redoubled to 32, and promptly rolled double 6s! The match was over in a single game.

Adapting your opening moves

In regular backgammon, you have different ways to play some of the opening moves. The situation's not quite the same in match play.

When you lead in a match, you don't normally want to introduce complications that can lead to gammons for either player. Steer for simple positions with little gammon potential.

Conversely, if you're trailing you need to seek complications and the opportunity to win a gammon.

In general, opening rolls that slot the 5-point or bring down builders, rather than splitting the back checkers, tend to lead to more gammons. When you split the back checkers early, you often make an advanced anchor and that significantly reduces your opponent's gammon chances.

Imagine you're winning 6–1 in a match to 9 and you win the opening roll with a 21. Moving 13/11, 24/23 is the right play. With this opening move, you're likely to end up in some sort of mutual holding game or a simple race. If you play 13/11, 6/5, the game is likely to be much more complex and you can end up in a prime-versus-prime position. (Turn to Chapter 8 for descriptions of the types of games.)

If you're trailing 1–6 and roll 21, then playing 13/11, 6/5 is mandatory because you want a complicated game.

Table 13-1 offers moves for opening rolls for leaders and trailers.

Table 13-1	Opening Rolls in Match Play	
Roll	*If You're Leading*	*If You're Trailing*
21	13/11, 24/23	13/11, 6/5
41	13/9, 24/23	13/9, 6/5
51	13/8, 24/23	13/8, 6/5
52	13/8, 24/22	13/8, 13/11
54	13/8, 24/20	13/8, 13/9
43	24/20, 13/10 (or 24/21, 13/9)	13/9, 13/10
32	24/21, 13/11	13/10, 13/11
64	24/14	24/18, 13/9 (or 8/2, 6/2)
52	13/8, 24/22	13/8, 13/11

The opening roll has a huge influence on what type of game you play so getting these moves correct is vital.

Concerning gammons

Gammons are very important in match play. When you're losing and win a gammon with the cube on 2 (or even better 4 or 8), you can quickly catch up.

Gammons are normally much more important for the trailer than the leader. When the leader wins a gammon, it may give him more points than he needs to win the match, but for the trailer it provides a great opportunity to get back in the match.

As the trailer, in order to win a gammon you can take a few more risks than you might take in a money game, because in a match the gains are worth the risk.

As Black, you lead 5–2 in a match to 7 and your opponent opens with a 62, which she plays 24/18, 13/11. You respond with 55 and play 8/3(2), 6/1(2)*. White rolls 61 and stays on the bar, leaving the position shown in Figure 13-2.

In a money game, you'd double this position and White would drop because you have a considerable gammon threat strong enough so that White does better by dropping.

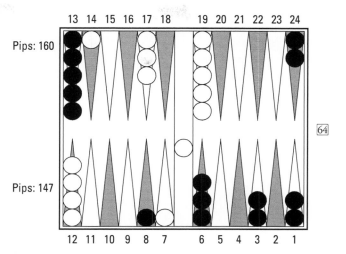

Figure 13-2: Losing a gammon is sometimes irrelevant.

But, in a match, if you're two points away from winning, and White takes the cube to 2, no difference exists for White between losing a single game and losing a gammon so the take is trivial because losing a gammon is irrelevant.

A double by you in this type of position is a gross error (but one I've seen made frequently). Your correct plan is to play on for an undoubled gammon. Those two points take you nicely to the winning score.

If you make the mistake and double, you give White what's known as a *free redouble*. If you double, White will redouble next move because if she loses the game she's going to lose the match anyway so she doesn't mind if the cube is on 2 or 4. But if White wins, she gains enormously from having the cube on 4. Indeed, if White were to win a gammon with the cube on 4, she, not you, wins the match, and you'll be seriously embarrassed.

In Figure 13-3, White runs out with an opening 64, playing 24/14 and as Black you use your 55 to make the hit on your 1-point and make your 3-point as well. This time the match score is 3–3 in a match to 7.

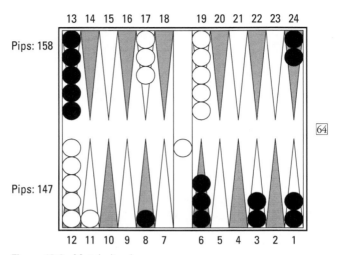

Figure 13-3: Matchplay drop.

In a money game, this benchmark position is well known to be a double and a take. Here, because you're exactly four points away from winning the match, a gammon with the cube on 2 gives you the match. Because of that, White does better to drop an offered double, go down 3-4, and play on from there.

The moral here is to beware of gammon positions when your opponent needs the exact number of points a gammon would give to win the match.

Figure 13-4 shows a slightly more complex example of match play tactics. As Black, you're losing 4–5 in a match to 7.

When you think about doubling in a tournament game, first consider what the correct actions would be in a money game. In the position in Figure 13-4 in money play, White would have enough chances to win and may take a double. If she enters quickly from the bar and can contain Black's back checker, she can later win with a redouble at the appropriate moment.

But, leading 5–4 in a tournament game, White can never win with a redouble as the two points she gets if she wins the game give her the match.

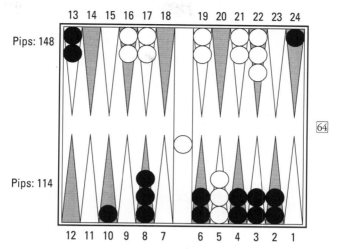

Figure 13-4: A complex match-play problem.

The inability to use the cube to win the game as you do in regular play makes a huge difference to how you play in a tournament game.

And, if White stays on the bar for a while, you could quite easily win a gammon and with it the match. These two factors combine to ensure that White must pass this double.

Be careful towards the end of a match as the doubling cube assumes characteristics not normally seen in money play. Consider particularly the threat of gammons and the usefulness of the doubling cube to you (or your opponent) at any specific match score. Too often I see players make cube decisions as if they were playing a money game. Remember that you're playing a match and that the score is the overriding factor in most doubling decisions.

Playing to the Score with Match Equity Tables

In the early days of tournament play the only difference between match and money play was that people were much tighter with the cube in matches, and it was rare to see the cube above 2.

Slowly but surely, players began to realise that the score has a significant influence on cube decisions. Ideas such as not doubling so readily when ahead in a match became standard. Soon, some of the keener minds decided to work out match equity tables.

The next sections are probably the most complex in the book, so I advise reading them several times.

Explaining a match equity table

A *match equity table* gives you the percentage chance of winning a match at any particular score.

In the late 1970s and early 1980s three players, Bill Robertie, Kit Woolsey, and Danny Kleinman, derived their own equity tables based on a mix of mathematical theory with a large amount of empirical evidence. Over the years, the method of constructing tables has become refined and the empirical evidence of real matches has greatly increased, so that now nearly universal agreement exists on the table values.

The important thing about the score in any match isn't how many points you have but how many points both players need in order to win the match. To read a match equity table, such as the one in Figure 13-5, which shows all possible scores in a nine-point match, you find where the number of points Black needs to win meets the number of points White needs to win. For example, if Black is leading White 7–3 in a match to 9, you go across Black's 2 row until it meets White's 6 column and see that Black's chances of winning are 81 per cent. The shorthand for Black needing two points and White needing six is needs 2 versus needs 6. The table gives the match-winning percentage from Black's viewpoint.

The advantage of defining the table in this way is that you can easily adapt it for shorter match lengths. For a five-point match, you just need the first five rows and columns.

White Needs

Black Needs	1	2	3	4	5	6	7	8	9
1	50	70	75	83	85	90	91	94	95
2	30	50	60	68	75	81	85	88	91
3	25	40	50	59	66	71	76	80	84
4	17	32	41	50	58	64	70	75	79
5	15	25	34	42	50	57	63	68	73
6	10	19	29	36	43	50	56	62	67
7	9	15	24	30	37	44	50	56	61
8	6	12	20	25	32	38	44	50	55
9	5	9	16	21	27	33	39	45	50

Figure 13-5: The 9-point match equity table.

Note: The percentages in the first column and first row apply to the Crawford Game when one or other player is at match point. After the Crawford Game is over, the match equity table isn't required because all doubling decisions are simple.

Calculating match equity tables

Unless you're a whizz with numbers you're likely to quickly forget the match equity table.

You can, however, calculate match equities by applying formulae. You can choose from at least four, including Neil's Numbers and the Underwood Formula, but I personally use the Janowski Formula, which is the one I explain here:

Let D = The difference between the two scores

Let T = The number of points the trailer needs to win the match

The Leader's Winning Chances (W) are:

$$50+\frac{(D\times 85)}{(T+6)}$$

Try this out on a score of 6–2 in a match to 9:

D = 4

T = 7

So, W = 50 + (4 × 85) / (7 + 6)

= 50 + 340 / 13

= 76 per cent (after rounding down)

You find the exact same number in the table entry for 'needs 3 needs 7'.

Note that the Janowski formula doesn't work for Crawford Game scores – you have to learn those separately.

I appreciate that this type of arithmetic isn't everyone's idea of fun, but don't worry – just understanding the concept of match equity will make you a better player than most of your peers even if you never calculate a match equity in your life!

Applying match equity tables

So, enough of the theory; time for a practical example. What could be simpler than the position shown in Figure 13-6? As Black, you own the cube on 2 and the score is tied at 3–3 in a match to 7. Should you redouble to 4 and put the match on the line? Should White take? In a money game this decision is easy. You should redouble and White, who has 28 per cent winning chances, should take.

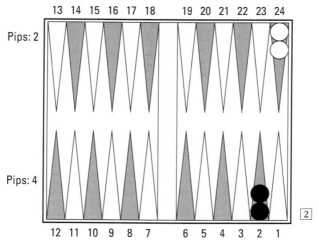

Figure 13-6: A match equity example.

Even in match play, I hope you can see that you must double. You're a 72 per cent favourite to win the game and therefore the match. For your opponent, the situation's different. If she takes she wins the game, and therefore the match, 28 per cent of the time. If she drops, you can use the match equity table to check her winning chances.

At 3–5 down (needs 4 versus needs 2) White's winning chances are 32 per cent. This percentage is 4 per cent better than her chances if she takes the double. In backgammon terms, 4 per cent is a huge difference. If she doesn't know about match equity tables. White could make a huge mistake here by accepting the redouble.

This example is a simple one to demonstrate the use of match equity tables. Of course, their use can be much more complicated but that is beyond the scope of this book. *How to Play Tournament Backgammon* by Kit Woolsey (Gammon Press) is a good source of further information if you want to study this topic in more depth. If you study Woolsey's book you can learn how to calculate take points at any match score. The standard 25 per cent take-point is no longer the norm, especially when one player has a big lead. I use some of these different take-points in the rest of this chapter without explaining how they're derived.

If you understand the concept of match equity, you're on the right road to becoming a good tournament player.

Nearing the end

The closer you get to the end of a match, the more critical it becomes to play to the score. Looking at all possible scores isn't feasible but I cover three important ones to give you some idea of tactics.

Needs 2 versus Needs 2

The least understood of all scores is when both players are two points away from winning the match. Whoever turns the cube first kills the cube and gammons. The game then becomes *Double Match Point* (DMP), and whoever wins the game wins the match. (I talk more about DMP in the next section.)

Always double if any chance exists that after the next exchange of rolls you can *lose your market*, that is, your opponent won't take your double next turn after a favourable sequence of your and your opponent's rolls.

Suppose your opponent's opening roll is 41 and she plays 13/9, 6/5. You must double! If you roll 44, hit both blots, and she can't get in on her next turn, you've lost your market, and White won't accept a double. Note that you don't gain anything by not doubling because if you don't hit the blot on her 5-point, she's going to double you. The only argument for not doubling in this situation is if you believe that your opponent doesn't understand the risk of losing her market, so by waiting you're giving her a chance to make a mistake of not doubling when she ought to and losing her market if things go well.

A lot of players don't like to put the match on the line and hold off from doubling in case things don't go well. This attitude is wrong. You must double if any possibility exists of losing your market by your next roll (and there nearly always is a sequence that will lose your market). Logically, if both players know what they're doing, this game is always the last game of the match. If you watch two good players in a match and they reach 2-away versus 2-away (another way of saying needs 2 versus needs 2), the doubling cube is always turned within the first two rolls of the game.

Note that the take point at this score is 30 per cent, much higher than the usual 25 per cent, and that is what dictates this strategy.

Needs 2 versus Needs 3

If you're leading 5–4 in a match to 7, you have a lead, but not a huge lead. You're at just 60 per cent to win in the equity table.

Adopt the following tactics:

> ✔ **As the leader:** If you have a gammon threat, play for an undoubled gammon rather than a doubled gammon. In non-gammon positions, the trailer can take if she has a 25 per cent chance to win – very similar to normal play. (If she drops the double she is at Needs 3, Needs 1 which is 25 per cent match winning chances – so this is the breakpoint for deciding whether or not to take the double. But note that the trailer can never win the game with the cube because she'll have already automatically redoubled to 4.) In other words, the game is played to a conclusion and the trailer never wins by redoubling the leader out as she has already redoubled to 4.

In a non-gammon position, as leader, you double as you would do in normal play.

✔ **As the trailer:** Double much earlier than usual as the leader's take point is 29 per cent rather than 25 per cent and she gets no value from holding the cube. If you have any sort of gammon threat, double even earlier.

In the 2007 World Championship Final, leading 23–22 in a game to 25, Alvaro Savio, playing Black, doubled Jorge Pan from the position shown in Figure 13-7. Doing so was a huge error. The position is gammon-ish because Black had good chances of executing a blitz so Savio should have played on for an undoubled gammon. On the next roll, Pan redoubled to 4 and thus gammons became irrelevant and the players effectively played this game for the title.

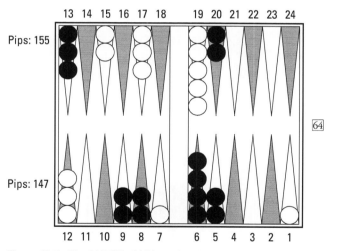

Figure 13-7: The 2007 World Championship.

Needs 4 versus Needs 2

If you're a double or redouble away from winning the match, apply the following set of tactics:

✔ **As the leader:** Rarely do you double at this score. The trailer's take point is low (17 per cent) and she'll redouble to 4 immediately to make optimal use of the four points she can win.

Your best plan is to play for an undoubled gammon.

> ✔ **As the trailer:** If you don't have a gammon threat, be slightly wary of doubling. The leader's take point is just 20 per cent and the two points would give her the match exactly.
>
> A gammon-ish position is different. The four points you can win give you the match so the leader is the one who has to be wary of taking.

In a money game, White (who's on roll) would double and as Black you've a comfortable take in the position shown in Figure 13-8. With Black leading 3–1 in a match to 5, you have a different story. As Black, you'd be making a huge blunder by taking. Gammons are great for White but irrelevant for you, so you don't get the full value of owning the cube. Also, you can never redouble White out and so you'll lose some games that you'd win in normal money play with a well-timed redouble.

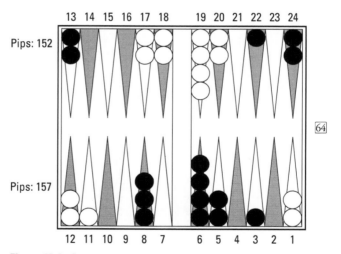

Figure 13-8: 2-away versus 4-away.

Double Match Point

Many matches come down to what's known as Double Match Point (DMP). Put simply, whoever wins the next game wins the match.

DMP can occur when both players are 1 point away from winning the match, but it can also occur when the cube reaches a level when whoever wins the next game wins the match. For example, in a match to 7 if the score is 5-4 and the cube is on 4, the situation is effectively DMP.

Obviously the doubling cube isn't in play and gammons and backgammons are irrelevant. Some general guidelines for playing at DMP:

  ✔ Keep all your checkers in play. For example, blitzes that make the 1-point early in the game are very committal so are not the game plan of choice. (Blitzes are one of the strategies I discuss in Chapter 8.)

  An army fights best when all soldiers are available for the battle. If some of your soldiers are stranded on your 1-point, they aren't on the front-line and you're potentially at a disadvantage if your opponent has all her checkers in active positions.

  ✔ Don't fear going into a back game. After all, you can't lose a gammon. If you can still have a strong home board after you hit a shot, a back game allows you to play more aggressively than usual.

  ✔ Hold an anchor in your opponent's home board longer than usual, because, again, you can't lose a gammon.

  ✔ Go with simple running plays. For example, playing 24/14 with an opening 64 roll is a good choice.

Figure 13-9 demonstrates quite clearly the difference between normal play and DMP play.

If this were a money game and you held the cube on 2, your correct play with this 64 would be to run one back checker with 23/13. You have good chances to save the gammon and with the checker you leave on the 23-point, you may be lucky to get a shot and then win the game.

At DMP a different story holds. Gammons are irrelevant, so you should hold the anchor and play your move in your home board. Your best move is 7/1, 6/2, which slots the two remaining open points in your board, and you can hope to close out your board next turn.

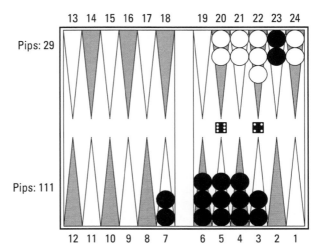

Figure 13-9: DMP play.

By holding the anchor, you get many more shots than if you run one checker.

As an example, look at the two different moves by Black and see how 33 plays for White after each.

Figure 13-10 shows another position from the 2007 World Championship final. At DMP, Savio, playing Black, played this 53 by moving bar/20, 4/1, which is the wrong move on two counts:

- ✓ When ahead in the race, you should race. Moving 4/1 doesn't advance him in the race.

- ✓ It takes a checker out of play. Playing 4/1 with the 3 takes that checker permanently out of play.

Savio should've played bar/20/17.

The game had an incredible end when Pan rolled 41 and correctly played 6/5*, 6/2. Savio then fanned for eight rolls in a row (!), by which time Pan was bearing off.

Of course backgammon wouldn't be the same game if apparent exceptions didn't exist. For my final discussion on DMP, I take you to November 2007 and the final of the first World Series of Backgammon tournament between John Hurst and Christian Plenz. In a tightly fought match, the players reached

DMP and deep into the final game the position was that shown in Figure 13-11.

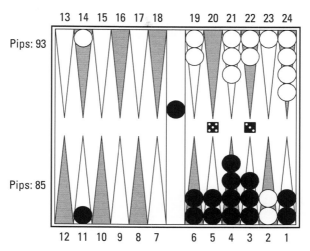

Figure 13-10: The 2007 World Championship (part 2).

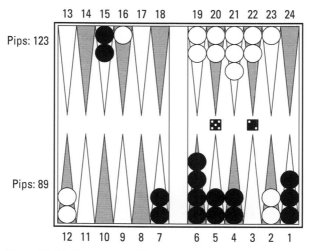

Figure 13-11: Hurst versus Plenz.

Plenz, playing Black, pondered long before moving 15/10, 15/13. He wanted to keep his checkers in play and didn't like the look of the safe play 6/1, 6/4.

He was wrong! White's home board was too strong for Plenz to be offering shots, and the safe play was the correct play. In this case, basic backgammon tactics should have won out over DMP considerations. Hurst rolled 65, played 23/12*, and went on to win the game.

Chapter 14

Using Computers and Online Play

In the modern world of backgammon, computers have had such a profound influence on the game that you need to look at how they can help you improve yours.

Playing Against Computers

You play the majority of your backgammon against other humans. One good reason for that situation is that they're far more sociable than the computer! However, in the modern world, if you really want to become a good player you need to know how to make use of computer programs.

The two most prominent backgammon programs are:

✔ **Snowie,** now in its fourth incarnation, and currently the most powerful commercial program available. Visit www. bgsnowie.com for information on cost and availability.

✔ **gnubg** is equally strong but has the advantage of being free. You can download it at www.gnubg.org.

Modern backgammon programs are known as *bots* – the shortened form of robots!

Welcome to the machine

For years a huge amount of investment poured into producing a chess program capable of beating a human being and it all paid off when IBM's Deep Blue beat the then world champion Gary Kasparov in 1997.

Given a powerful computer, such as Deep Blue, the sheer processing power of the machine ensures that it nearly always finds the best move. As computers become ever more powerful, so their playing strength improves.

The same investment that went into Deep Blue wasn't available for backgammon programmers so the development of a good program took far longer.

Chess programs work in a relatively straightforward manner. Given an initial position they look at all future possible positions so many moves ahead, evaluate all those possible moves based on a set of pre-programmed criteria, and choose the move that has the highest rating. This method is known as *tree search*.

Tree search doesn't work so well for backgammon because far more possible moves exist in backgammon each turn than in chess as a result of the variability introduced by the dice.

Computers aren't yet powerful enough to produce a strong backgammon program based on tree search. However, that knowledge hasn't stopped people trying and all the early programs were based on this technique.

An early success did occur in 1979 when Hans Berliner's Gammonoid actually beat the then World Champion, Luigi Villa, in a short match. However, the program was quite lucky with its dice rolls.

Matters took a giant leap forward in the early 1990s when a scientist, Dr Gerry Tesauro, began to use neural networks. His idea was to produce a computer capable of more accurately modelling the human brain in its working. Neural network theory involves giving a computer the basics of a problem and then letting it work out how to solve the problem itself, rather than hard coding algorithms into it.

For Tesauro, backgammon was the perfect testing vehicle. He taught his program, TD-Gammon, the rules of backgammon and then told it to work out for itself the best strategy and tactics. By playing half a million games against itself, it did just that.

The end result was fascinating as some of the plays that humans had thought for decades were correct were shown to be errors! That TD-Gammon was no idiot was proved quickly when the best players of the day only just showed a slight edge when playing long sessions against it.

Not long after TD-Gammon came the first commercial neural net backgammon program, JellyFish, created by Frederik Dahl.

Today's neural net programs, Snowie and gnubg, are as strong as the best players in the world.

Not everyone can find a willing backgammon partner. Jon Royset, the 2003 World Champion, lives north of the Arctic Circle in Norway where he couldn't find many good players. He spent a couple of years playing against computers to hone his game and then surprised everyone by carrying off the ultimate prize in Monte Carlo.

Mousing to move

If you're familiar with computers you won't have any trouble playing against backgammon computer programs. The board is clearly represented in two-dimensional or three-dimensional form and all interaction between you and the computer is performed using the mouse. A dice roll is but a mouse click and you drag the checkers to their new destination using the mouse.

Not all programs are identical so I don't describe a standard method here but you can pick up the idea quickly once you get started. Similarly, as all programs display their boards in graphic colour I can't show you a copy in a black-and-white book!

One useful facet of computer play is that the pip count for both sides is constantly on display so that detail's one less thing you have to worry about!

Finding your level

To start with, just play a few games against the program to get used to playing while looking at a screen. Although doing so sounds easy, adapting does take a while and you may find that you miss moves that you'd see over a physical board. I offer no explanation for this situation – the human mind just works this way!

Nearly all programs can play at different strengths, for example beginner, novice, intermediate, expert, and so on. The playing strengths reflect how far the program looks ahead, measured in terms of 'ply':

> ✓ A 1-ply look ahead means looking at the computer's next move and making a judgement on what's the best move.

> ✔ A 2-ply look ahead means looking at one computer move and the opponent's possible replies and then making a judgement.

> ✔ A 3-ply look ahead means looking at the computer's first move, the opponent's possible replies, and the next computer move before making a judgement.

The more plays used, the stronger the computer becomes.

In the bad old days (in computer terms, the 1990s) the processing power of computers put severe limitations on the number of plys used in live play. Nowadays, however, you can play in 3-ply all the time if you want to.

If you're a beginner, start off with one of the computer's weaker playing styles and then as you progress adjust the strength as you wish.

Unlike the early computers, today's programs are very strong so don't get depressed if you get beaten! Many people think that computers cheat by throwing the right dice at the right time but the rolls are randomly generated and the programs definitely don't cheat.

Computers are strong because:

> ✔ Modern, neural-net programs have taken their basic playing strength to high standards.

> ✔ They never overlook a play.

> ✔ They always play the logically correct play.

> ✔ They have no emotions so don't get influenced by what happened in previous games.

Taking hints

Some programs have a useful facility enabling you to ask for a hint if you're not sure of which play to choose.

Playing using hints is really helpful. Taking the time to work out *why* the computer recommended a certain play is even better. You learn far more quickly if you take the time to think things through.

Figure 14-1 offers a fairly difficult example to make my point.

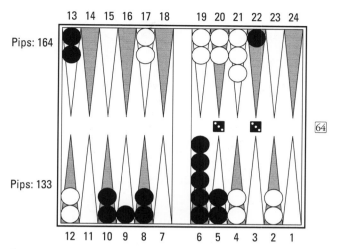

Figure 14-1: Taking hints.

As a relative beginner, you've got into this complex position. Your opponent is playing a back game and you've just thrown double 3s. As ever with small doubles, many different ways exist to play them. You've at least four reasonable plays:

✔ 10/7(2), 6/3(2)

✔ 9/6, 6/3(3)

✔ 10/7(2), 9/3

✔ 13/7(2)

And you probably have a few more moves that aren't blunders. Now's a good time to ask the computer to help you. It tells you that the first play is the best play and, comfortable in the knowledge that the computer's not leading you into a trap, you make your move!

(The reason 10/7(2), 6/3(2) is the best play is that it makes the best use of the spare checkers on the 6-point and also makes a 4-point prime.)

Going for analysis

Even if you don't take the hints after you play each move, you can still ask the computer to help you analyse moves.

Checking your equity

Computer programs look at things in terms of equity. Put simply, *equity* is the likelihood of winning or losing. An equity of 1 represents a certain win and –1 is a certain loss. In backgammon things get complicated by gammons and backgammons and so you can have an equity of 2, which is a certain gammon win, or even 3 for a certain backgammon win.

For each move, Snowie gives you two lines of information:

- ✔ The first line shows the number of plys used to evaluate the positions (normally 3), the move itself, and the expected equity outcome for the move.
- ✔ The second line tells you the percentages of backgammons, gammons (including backgammons) and total wins that you can expect to win and lose after each move.

You can do a great deal with this information but for now I only look at equity.

Looking at the equity of your chosen move and the difference between that and the equity of the best play (unless of course you chose the best play) is the key. In computer program terms, an equity difference of 0.03 or more is classed as an error and a difference of 0.11 or more is a blunder.

Avoiding blunders is the way to become a good backgammon player. Figure 14-2 shows Snowie's evaluation of the ten best plays available with a 33 roll in the position shown in Figure 14-1. It shows that any move other than 10/7(2), 6/3(2) is actually a blunder – certainly not something that's obvious at first sight, even to an expert!

Improve your game and your understanding by studying the equity difference between the various plays and working out why one move is better than another. At first doing so is difficult but becomes second nature as you improve.

1.	3	10/7(2) 6/3(2)		0.477				
		1.7%	22.3%	60.7%	39.3%	10.8%	0.6%	
2.	3	9/6 6/3(3)		0.336	(-0.141)			
		1.4%	20.5%	58.1%	41.9%	10.9%	0.5%	
3.	3	10/7(2) 9/3		0.283	(-0.195)			
		1.3%	19.7%	57.2%	42.8%	12.9%	0.6%	
4.	3	13/7(2)		0.281	(-0.196)			
		1.2%	18.4%	57.0%	43.0%	11.4%	0.6%	
5.	3	13/10(2) 6/3(2)		0.207	(-0.270)			
		1.3%	19.0%	55.0%	45.0%	12.7%	0.7%	
6.	3	13/10 9/6 6/3(2)		0.193	(-0.284)			
		1.2%	18.8%	54.7%	45.3%	12.8%	0.7%	
7.	3	13/10(2) 9/3		0.042	(-0.435)			
		1.0%	16.7%	51.7%	48.3%	14.5%	0.7%	
8.	3	8/5(2) 6/3(2)		-0.027	(-0.504)			
		1.2%	18.5%	48.9%	51.1%	15.6%	0.8%	
9.	3	13/10 10/7(3)		-0.077	(-0.554)			
		1.1%	16.4%	48.9%	51.1%	16.6%	0.9%	
10.	3	9/3 8/5 6/3		-0.166	(-0.643)			
		1.2%	17.3%	46.3%	53.7%	18.4%	1.0%	

Figure 14-2: Snowie's ranking of the ten best plays for Figure 14-1.

Sleeping soundly with computer confirmation

One huge advantage of computers is that you can use them to check your plays after the event. Suppose you played at your local club in a big chouette and at a critical point you had to make a decision between two plays; you chose one, lost the game, and ended up a big loser on the night.

Without computers you'd spend a sleepless night wondering about that play but putting the position into Snowie or gnubg and finding out whether you made a hideous blunder or whether the dice just weren't with you is a moment's work.

Figure 14-3 shows a critical point against four opponents. You have to decide between moving 9/1 or playing your 62 roll by moving 15/9, 15/13. Because you can't see how to get those checkers home safely from your 15-point if you play 9/1, you choose 15/9, 15/13. (This situation is known as a *pay me now, pay me later* play because you can take a small risk now to avoid a big risk later.)

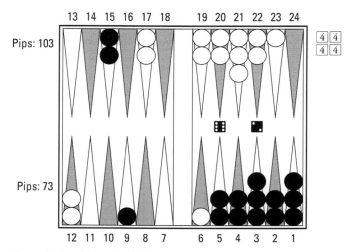

Figure 14-3: Making the right move but getting the wrong result.

Your opponents roll 21, play 13/12*, 4/2, and win with a redouble on their next turn after you fan your re-entry chance with 66. You realise that had you played 9/1 with your earlier 62, the double 6s would've won you the game.

But, plugging the data into Snowie or gnubg, you discover that 15/9, 15/13 is the right play by a big margin – you were just unlucky on the night. You go to sleep a wiser, if poorer, person!

Setting the computer to do rollouts

Although computer 3-ply evaluations are good, they're not infallible. Doing a rollout is the most accurate way to evaluate a position.

A *rollout* is literally what it says. From a given position during a game, you roll out the position until you reach the end of the game and note down who wins and what type of game is won (single/gammon/backgammon). So instead of looking only three moves ahead and then evaluating the position (3-ply look ahead) you actually complete the whole game.

You repeat this process (at least) once for each possible dice roll to even out the luck on the first roll (which is often critical). Thus rollouts are normally done in batches of 36.

The best players learn a lot from doing manual rollouts and rollouts certainly help to improve the overall level of play. They are, however, extremely tedious! Rollouts consume hours of time and, although they can give a good idea of the right play, the number of rollouts aren't sufficient to provide statistical accuracy.

Luckily computers came along and by their very nature are ideally suited for doing rollouts. Now, you can ask your computer to rollout a position literally thousands of times while you sleep.

The results from computer rollouts are very accurate and you can be 99 per cent certain that they show you the correct play in any particular position.

I asked Snowie to rollout the top two plays for the 33 roll in the position in the first figure in this chapter – Figure 14-1. Figure 14-4 shows its answers.

Note that the '3' in the first line (indicating a 3-ply analysis) of Figure 14-2 has now been replaced with an 'R' (showing the results are based on a rollout). Note also that the percentages of the different types of game won and lost differ from the original 3-ply analysis.

1. R   10/7(2) 6/3(2)   0.410
        1.6%   22.1%   59.5%   40.5%   11.4%   0.5%
2. R   9/6 6/3(3)   0.315   (-0.096)
        1.8%   20.9%   57.1%   42.9%   10.8%   0.5%

Figure 14-4: Snowie rollout.

The ranking remains the same but the equity figures are different from those in Figure 14-2. Sometimes the rankings change and a move that was the first choice after a 3-ply evaluation is demoted after a rollout.

Rollouts are frequently used to evaluate doubling decisions. A position that was initially evaluated as double/take becomes double/pass after a rollout, and vice versa.

Computer rollouts are powerful and have done more than anything else to help the development of the game in the last ten years. Use them wisely and they can help your game a lot!

Venturing Online

Once the Internet arrived, it didn't take long for people to work out that being able to play online, against each other or against a computer, would be fun.

Today you can choose from hundreds of sites that provide online games. (I offer tips for finding websites in the 'Playing Online' section later in this chapter.) Most of these sites enable you to test yourself against a computer even if you don't have the necessary software on your own.

Before playing online, I strongly recommend playing against Snowie or gnubg first. Playing on a computer is very different to live play and you need to be comfortable with playing using a mouse and seeing the board vertically in front of you rather than playing in the traditional way.

Nearly all online sites offer three types of play: for fun, for money, and tournament play, which normally involves money as well. I recommend playing a few games for fun before wagering any money on the outcome. Once you're comfortable with the human–computer interface (HCI), then and only then start playing for money.

Thousands of people never play for money on the Internet. They're happy just to play their favourite game with other enthusiasts across the world.

Watching others

Most sites let you watch matches between other players. Before you play at all, watching others in action is a good idea. Certainly if you're new to online play, observing is the best way to get acclimatised to the whole idea.

Being able to watch online offers the huge advantage of studying some of the world's top players. You can benefit hugely from observing the best in action.

Occasionally, matches such as the World Championship final are broadcast via one of the online sites with commentary by a top-class player using the Chat facility. Live broadcasts are not only great entertainment, they also provide one of the best ways to get a really good understanding of top-level tournament play.

You're given the option of making your games private so no one can watch them. If you want to hide your playing style from the general public, you can do so!

Paying the rake

In the early days of online play, many sites charged a subscription fee, but in today's competitive world the subscription model has all but disappeared. Generally, if you play for fun no fee is charged. The sites earn their revenue by charging a *rake* – a percentage of the winnings or tournament entry fees – from the money players.

If you're playing online for £10 a point and win a doubled game against your opponent, you normally bank £20. Online you bank slightly less than that because the site takes a percentage from each game. Typically the rake is between 2 and 5 per cent, although it can vary quite significantly. The winner of a game pays the rake for both winner and loser.

In a tournament, the rake is taken from your entry fee. As an example, you pay £44 to enter a tournament, as do nine other players, giving a total pot of £440. Typically, the website keeps £40 and the prize pool is actually £400.

Playing at speed

In a normal everyday game no time limit is placed on your play – except increasingly in tournaments. Online this situation wouldn't work so time limits have to be set.

As per tournament play you get a bank of time – typically two minutes – and an allowance per move, say thirty seconds. If you run out of time, you lose the game. (Chapter 13 talks more about clocks and tournament play.)

Most sites offer two and sometimes three speeds of play. A very fast game is 15 seconds per play, with a bank of one minute. Playing at that speed certainly keeps you focused!

Chatting

The chat feature is a facility common to all sites. You can converse with your opponent as you play, making the whole thing a bit friendlier.

Sometimes your opponent may take exception to your luck (when, of course, your skill alone has enabled you to beat him) and send the odd rude note but generally the chat feature enhances the game and enables you to talk about backgammon to people all over the world.

Cheating

In a perfect world, cheating wouldn't happen. However, in the real world, wherever money's involved, unscrupulous people go to great lengths to try to separate you from it by fair means or foul. Fair means is fine but we need to stop the foul!

To cheat online, the player or an accomplice asks a computer what the right move is every time they throw the dice. They then use the computer's suggested play on every move. As computers are very good, this process produces wins most of the time.

A number of players used this method in the early days of online play and made a lot of money doing so. However, what humans can invent humans can also circumvent and the online sites didn't take long to develop software that tracks each player's moves and compares them with the moves a computer would make. This software has become highly sophisticated and cheating online is extremely difficult. If you couple this software protection with playing at a fairly fast speed, it becomes all but impossible to cheat.

Despite the protection from cheating, I still recommend that you keep high-stake games for face-to-face play. Use the Internet as a training ground and play for sensible stakes rather than trying to make your living by playing for hundreds of pounds per game.

Playing Online

So you're ready to play – what do you do next? The answers are in the next sections.

Choosing a site

First, you need to decide where to play. Everyone has their personal preferences but here are a few things to consider when choosing an online site:

- ✔ Has the site been recommended to you?

- ✔ Is the user interface easy to use? Look for good graphics and clear directions for moving the checkers and making doubling decisions.

- ✔ How much is the rake, or percentage, the site keeps? (This detail is a key criterion for most players.)

- ✔ Can you always get a game? All sites have 24/7 availability but are enough people playing day and night to ensure that you don't have to wait to get a game?

- ✔ Does it occasionally add money to its tournament prize funds?

- ✔ Does it have a good support system? Most sites are stable but if you have problems they need to be quickly resolved by expert personnel.

- ✔ Do good players use the site? You have to establish this by repute as most players use a pseudonym online.

- ✔ Is it easy to deposit and withdraw funds?

You don't have to limit yourself to one site. Try a few and see which you prefer. I know many players who regularly use two or three sites, sometimes playing simultaneously on two or more (not recommended for the faint-hearted!).

Choosing a stake

In everyday backgammon you can't set a limit on how much you might win or lose in any one game. But online you don't have unlimited funds. When you start playing for money, you deposit funds with the site and the site then administers those funds like a bank account, adding in your wins and subtracting your losses.

To cope with the risk of large losses, you must define two things whenever you play:

- ✓ The amount of the basic stake.
- ✓ Your maximum win/loss amount.

If you're playing for £10 per point you can set your maximum win/loss at £20, £40, £80, £160, and so on. The maximum amount is normally (but not always) a possible value of the cube times the basic stake. For example (£10, £80) means a basic stake of £10 and a maximum loss of £80. That £80 covers a gammon loss with the cube on 4 but remember that if you lose a gammon with the cube on 8, you still only pay £80.

You can also set your maximum loss to be the basic stake, that is, £10. If you do so, you're effectively playing a single game for the nominal stake with gammons and backgammons not counting. If you're keen on tournament play, this approach is an excellent way to practise playing at Double Match Point. (Chapter 13 has information about how to play when the winner of the next game wins it all.)

Your maximum loss can't exceed the funds in your account. For example, if you only have £50 in your account you won't be allowed to play in a game where the maximum loss is £80 – you must find a lower-stakes game or top up your account.

Choosing an opponent

Starting a game online is easy. You challenge someone listed as willing to play (with stake and limit defined) or you set up a new game and wait for someone to challenge you. Challenges may be accepted or declined, and after each game finishes you have the option to continue the session or not – all polite and mannerly.

When you first venture online, you're unknown and your potential opponents are unknown to you. Luckily most sites operate a rating system and every game you play contributes to that rating. Ratings are based on the system originally worked out by Arpad Elo for chess and known (not surprisingly) as *Elo ratings*. I won't go into detail here but when you start playing online, you're given a rating of 1,500. The best players and the best bots in the world have ratings of around 1,900. A difference of 200 means that the person with the higher rating is significantly better.

You choose opponents, and they can choose you, based on ratings. Playing for large stakes against someone with a rating of more than 100 greater than you is unwise but if you can get a game at low stakes against better players, doing so is an excellent way to develop your game at low costs.

Of course, as you play regularly on a site it becomes just like any other club – you know who you want to play against and whom to avoid.

Varying your tactics online

Winnings and losses having set limits leads to slightly different tactics online because the limits can affect your handling of the doubling cube.

In a money game with White on roll, he'd double and, as Black, you'd drop in the position shown in Figure 14-5.

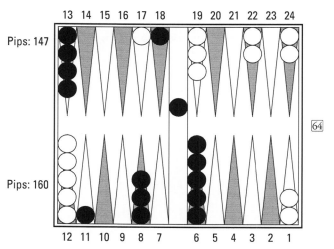

Figure 14-5: Setting limits can free up your play.

Now suppose that you're playing for £10 a point and your maximum win/loss is set at £20. White doubles – do you take? The answer is yes. The only reason the position is normally a drop is that you lose too many gammons but in this position you can't really lose a gammon. Yes, your opponent can gammon you but instead of collecting £40, he only collects £20 because you both agreed to the £20 limit. Effectively, gammons don't count. This fact turns a marginal drop into an easy take.

In standard play, the position in Figure 14-6 is a redouble and take. White can take because if you roll a 1, he can redouble to 8 and you must take because your winning chances are above 25 per cent.

Now consider an online game where you play for £10 with a £40 limit. You still offer a redouble to 4 but if your opponent takes, he's making a big error because if you roll a 1 he can't redouble you – the game already reached its limit with your redouble to 4.

Subtle differences such as this one abound in online play because of the artificial limits that have to be put in place. The vast majority of online players don't understand these differences. By applying this knowledge, you can make a considerable (positive) impact on your winnings.

You're ready to play online – good luck!

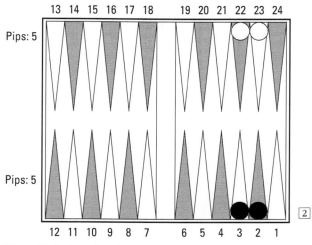

Figure 14-6: An online drop.

Part V
The Part of Tens

The 5th Wave · By Rich Tennant

'Excuse me. This was supposed to be a chouette - not a scrum.'

In this part . . .

No *For Dummies* book is complete without the Part of Tens, a little batch of small but perfectly-formed chapters listing ten things each. Here you'll find books for further study, useful backgammon resources, and my own personal ten backgammon commandments.

Chapter 15

The Ten Commandments of Backgammon

*Y*ou apply a set of basic tactics and strategies to playing any game or sport. Backgammon is no exception and in this chapter I provide a synopsis of the key tactics and strategies that can help you to play the game well.

Thou shalt Love the Game Above All Others and Have no Other Game but Backgammon

I say this tongue in cheek but I have loved and studied the game for over 30 years. Here are just a few of the quotes that have inspired my fascination with backgammon:

> ✔ 'We don't stop playing because we grow old, we grow old because we stop playing.' – George Bernard Shaw

> ✔ 'Life organised too well becomes monotonous; too much peace and security breed boredom.' – A. A. Brill

🡒 'The race is not always to the swift or the battle to the strong – but that's the way to bet.' – Damon Runyan

🡒 'Backgammon, like love, like music, has the power to make people happy.' – Siegbert Tarrasch (paraphrased)

Thou shalt Follow the Words of the Expert Magriel

Many years ago Paul Magriel set down some basic questions that you can ask yourself to determine the correct approach in any given situation. These questions have stood the test of time and I still use them today.

Tactical questions are:

🡒 Do you hold an advanced point (anchor) in your opponent's board (normally her 4-point or 5-point)? Having an advanced point enables you to play boldly. (Refer to Chapter 7 for strategies with anchors.)

🡒 How strong is your opponent's inner board? The stronger your opponent's inner board, the more conservatively you must play. (Chapter 6 talks about structure.)

🡒 How strong is *your* inner board (especially compared to your opponent's)? If you have more inner board points closed than your opponent, you tend to play boldly; with fewer points closed, more conservatively.

🡒 Does your opponent have blots in her inner board? If so, you can afford to take more chances because of possible return shots.

Magriel's strategic questions include:

🡒 How many checkers do you have back? The more you have back in your opponent's home board, the more chances you can take. The reason is that by adding one more checker you very likely make little difference but with no checkers back or only one back, you must play more conservatively.

✔ How many checkers does your opponent have back? When she has none or only one checker back, play provocatively to try to force an exchange of hits.

Thou shalt do Thy Sums

You cannot become a great player without doing some arithmetic. As a reminder:

✔ 36: Possible rolls of two dice

✔ 11: Rolls that contain a specific number

✔ 20: Rolls that contain any two specific numbers

✔ 27: Rolls that contain any three specific numbers

✔ 32: Rolls that contain any four specific numbers

✔ 35: Rolls that contain any five specific numbers

Become familiar with doing pip counts and then apply the 10 per cent rule (both covered in Chapter 5) or preferably the 8-9-12 rule (see Chapter 9) for doubling decisions.

Thou shalt Hit in the Openings

Many players are loath to hit and expose blots in the opening, but the opening defines the course of the whole game. If the best play involves hitting, so be it.

In Figure 15-1, White opened with 62 and played 24/18, 13/11. You, as Black, now roll 52. The correct play is 6/1*, 24/22. Taking half of White's next roll away (she must use it to enter) and making a lot of her rolls containing a 6 poor for her next turn are more important than anything else.

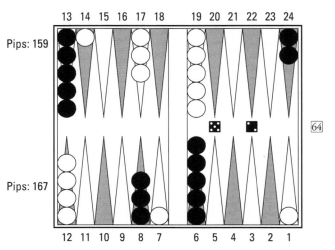

Figure 15-1: Hitting early.

Thou shalt not Kill (the Checkers)

Backgammon is played with 15 foot-soldiers (checkers) in each army. When you put a checker on a point where it cannot join in the fight, you place your army at a disadvantage. Try to keep your checkers in play and contributing to the battle. Figure 15-2 shows a straightforward example.

You could play 4/1 with your 21 roll, leaving no shots. But this isn't the time for that checker on your 4-point to slope off for a rest. He needs to stay in the line of fire on behalf of his fellow soldiers.

If White doesn't roll a 4, you can hope to complete your home board next turn and then escape your two back checkers in complete safety. The correct play is 8/5.

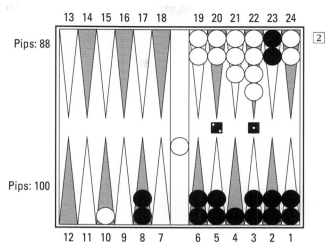

Figure 15-2: Using the whole army.

Thou shalt not Take a Knife to a Gunfight

Butch Cassidy wouldn't take on a gunslinger with just a knife and neither should you. As in life, times occur in backgammon when leading with your chin isn't right.

In other words, don't provoke a fight when you're at a disadvantage. You're better off consolidating your position and waiting for reinforcements rather than trying to slug it out when you're at a numerical or tactical disadvantage.

The situation in Figure 15-3 clarifies the point. The game has not started well for you as Black, and now you have to play this 41. You could play bar/20 with the idea of establishing an anchor next turn.

However, this play is the proverbial knife to a gunfight. White will attack you somewhere next turn and, as she has the better board, she's favoured to come out ahead in any exchange.

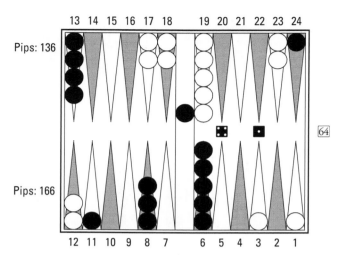

Figure 15-3: If you don't have the firepower, don't go looking for a fight.

Although it may seem timid, the correct play is bar/24, 13/9. That ace-point anchor keeps you in the game forever and if White doesn't hit one of your blots next turn, you'll have a good chance to establish a strong position on your own side of the board.

Thou shalt Remember that Every Roll is a Doubling Decision

More points are surrendered through poor doubling decisions than anything else in backgammon. If you handle the doubling cube well, you're likely to be a winner.

At the start of each turn, think of the doubling cube if you currently own it or the cube is in the middle. Positions change quickly, so you must constantly re-evaluate your options. What may have been an easy no double or a clear take a few moments ago may now be a chance to offer a double and prompt your opponent to drop.

Don't be afraid to wield the cube – who knows how your opponent's going to react when she sees it resting on 8 in the middle of the board awaiting her decision. As Karl von Clausewitz, the Prussian military thinker, famously said: 'Given the same amount of intelligence, timidity will do a thousand times more damage than audacity.'

Giving your opponent the chance to make a mistake is never wrong. If you think along the lines of, 'I'll just take a roll and see what happens', by next turn you may have missed your opportunity.

Take the position in Figure 15-4. If you, as Black, roll a 6, you can play on to try for a gammon, while still being able to double your opponent out any time. If you stay on the bar and White rolls a 6, she becomes favourite.

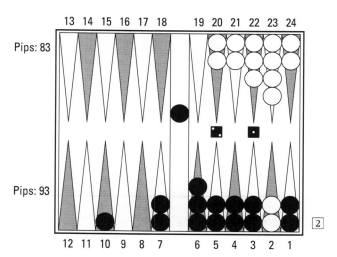

Figure 5-4: Seizing the moment to double.

The position is highly volatile and now is precisely the right moment to give White a difficult decision. Despite the fact that the position is a take, I know a lot of players would drop a redouble here. What a simple way to win two points.

Backgammon is all about applying pressure and this position graphically demonstrates that principle.

Thou shalt Use the Proper Tools to Evaluate Thy Doubling Decisions

Because doubling decisions are so crucial to backgammon, taking that little bit longer over them than you do over other plays is always worthwhile.

Having a method to help you evaluate your positions is also crucial. In this book I cover two methods:

- ✔ **Reference positions:** You accumulate a library of positions you've seen before and for which you know the right doubling decision. You constantly build on this library and re-use the information within it. On being presented with a new position, always check out your reference library to see what similar positions you have on file! (I talk more about reference positions in Chapter 5.)

- ✔ **SRT (Structure, Race, Threat):** In Chapter 6 I outline how to evaluate positions using the three basic criteria of structure, race, and threat. Base your analysis on these three elements before you consider other things such as psychology and match score.

Figure 15-5 shows references in action. This situation is certainly a double for Black – one good roll for him and White won't be able to take next time.

Using the race formulae, White would have a drop but she can win games by hitting a shot as Black attempts to bear in his checkers. The question is whether her racing plus her shot chances get her to 25 per cent winning chances (the Holy Grail number to accept a double in backgammon).

Exact calculation is impossible, so just knowing that this position is a take and filing it in your reference library is easier. Move the three checkers on Black's 10-point to his 9-point and the position becomes a double for Black and a drop for White.

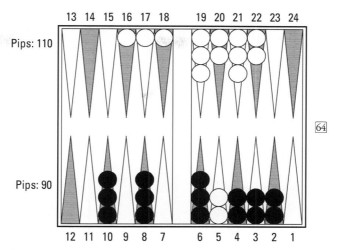

Figure 15-5: Putting reference positions to work.

Sadly for the student of the game, small changes can make quite a difference in the evaluation of a position. For this reason, becoming really good at backgammon takes years – you've such a lot to discover!

Thou shalt not Play on Automatic

Playing without thinking and making mistakes without noticing them is just too easy. Each position has its own idiosyncrasies and attention to detail is necessary if you're to play to your full potential.

As Black and playing on automatic in Figure 15-6, you would quickly play 24/13 and pick up your dice, happy to have escaped your rearmost checker.

But hang on a minute; you're behind in the race by 14 pips even after that play. What is your game plan? Trying to win the race doesn't look correct. Have another look.

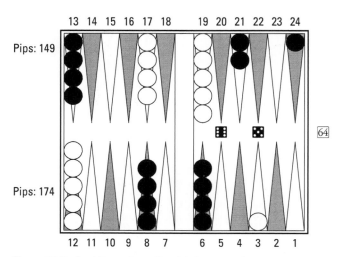

Figure 15-6: Avoiding automatic mistakes.

That rear checker needs to stay where it is to make White's rolls as awkward as possible. Meanwhile White has a single back checker. Consider the rule: 'Attack a blot, prime an anchor.' Following these two strategies leads you to the correct play: 13/7, 8/3*!

So a little clear thinking and the application of your backgammon knowledge lead you to the right play – backgammon's an easy game when you use your skills.

Thou shalt Study and Play both Humans and Bots

As champion golfer Gary Player once said, 'The more I practise, the luckier I get.' You can take that maxim and apply it to any game but particularly backgammon. You don't get better by luck; you get better through a mixture of study and play.

My guidelines for rapid improvement are:

- ✔ Play a lot against a range of different opponents.
- ✔ Read at least one book on backgammon theory every six months (I list a few in Chapter 16).

    When I bought my first one – *The Backgammon Book* by Jacoby and Crawford (Viking Press) – it opened up a whole new world for me. When I bought and studied my second book – *Backgammon for Profit* by Joe Dwek (Stein and Day) – I started to beat people who'd regularly beaten me. What a sense of satisfaction!

- ✔ Play different people.
- ✔ Play (and analyse) using the computer programs Snowie and gnubg (head to Chapter 16 for more on these).
- ✔ Play chouettes (I explain this multi-player version in Chapter 12).
- ✔ Play online (I list a few websites in Chapter 16).
- ✔ Play tournaments and matches (check Chapter 13 for info on tournament play).

If you manage to follow these guidelines, you can quickly develop your game. Balance studying with playing and get as much enjoyment out of the game as I have over the last 30 years.

I'll leave the last word to William Shakespeare: 'The play's the thing.'

Chapter 16

Ten Useful Backgammon Resources

A multitude of resources is available to the aspiring backgammon player. This chapter contains details of ten of them.

Top Ten Books

Here, in alphabetical order, are the ten most useful backgammon books for you to read along with *Backgammon For Dummies:*

- ✔ *Advanced Backgammon: Volumes 1 and 2*, Bill Robertie (Gammon Press)

- ✔ *Backgammon*, Paul Magriel (Quadrange/*New York Times*)

- ✔ *Backgammon Boot Camp*, Walter Trice (Fortuitous Press)

- ✔ *Backgammon Praxis*, Marty Storer (Fortuitous Press)

- ✔ *Classic Backgammon Revisited*, Jeremy Bagai (Flaming Sparrow Press)

- ✔ *How to Play Tournament Backgammon*, Kit Woolsey (Gammon Press)

- *Modern Backgammon*, Bill Robertie (Gammon Press)
- *The Backgammon Encyclopaedia: Vol 1*, Kit Woolsey (Gammon Press)
- *Vision Laughs at Counting with Advice to the Dicelorn*, Danny Kleinman (Randolph Strommen)
- *What Colour is the Wind?*, Chris Bray (Chris Bray)

Online Supply Sources

You need somewhere to buy books, boards, dice, and other backgammon paraphernalia. Consider these:

- **The Backgammon Shop:** Offering one of the best places to buy your backgammon provisions at www.bgshop.com.
- **Backgammon a la Carte:** This site is run by Carol Joy Cole (see the later section 'Flint Area Backgammon News'). Visit www.flintbg.com/boutique.html.
- **The Gammon Village Store:** You can find an excellent selection of backgammon goods at www.gammonvillage.com.

Auction Websites

For buying new or second-hand backgammon boards or precision dice or a whole host of other backgammon-related goods, online auction sites can be cost-effective. Auction websites include www.ebay.co.uk, www.ebid.net, and www.webidz.com.

Flint Area Backgammon News

Carol Joy Cole has been one of the driving forces behind backgammon in America for many years. As well as producing a monthly printed newsletter, *Flint Area Backgammon News*, that's distributed all over the world, she helps to run many tournaments and has made Flint one of the focal points for the game in the USA.

Carol keeps an excellent stock of books, boards, and backgammon accessories, which you can order at www.flintbg.com.

Chicago Point

Bill Davis is the other mainstay of backgammon in the USA. Like Carol Joy Cole (see preceding section), he also produces a monthly magazine, *Chicago Point*. His website, www.chicagopoint.com, contains a wealth of backgammon information, such as the history of doubling and an archive of photos from the last 40 years featuring such luminaries as Paul Magriel and Prince Alexis Obolensky, the man who created the modern tournament circuit.

In addition, one of Bill's colleagues, Mel Leifer, maintains the Chicago Point links site at www.chicagopoint.com/links.html. This site is probably the single most useful backgammon website as it provides links to hundreds of other backgammon-centric websites, giving you information on clubs around the world, backgammon publications, tournament schedules, and so on.

Backgammon Software

Two world-class backgammon computer programs can help you improve your game:

- ✔ **Snowie** is the commercial version. Details can be found at www.bgsnowie.com.
- ✔ **gnubg** is a free program produced by the gnu foundation. You can download it from www.gnubg.org.

In terms of playing strength, the two programs are virtually identical. Snowie (in my opinion) has the slightly better user interface but gnubg has one or two useful features not found in Snowie.

Online Playing Sites

Mel Leifer's links page at www.chicagopoint.com/links.html directs you to most of the websites where you can play backgammon online. Try a few to see which ones suit you. I regularly use two sites:

- ✔ Ladbrokes, `http://backgammon.ladbrokes.com/en`, has one of the lowest rakes on the Internet. (The *rake* is the amount that the site deducts from your winnings as a fee for using the site.)

- ✔ Partygammon, `www.partygammon.com`, has a nice user interface and runs a good number of regular tournaments.

US laws currently prohibit the use of online gaming sites by American citizens. I have no doubt these laws will be repealed in due course; the only question is when.

BIBA

In the UK, the British Isles Backgammon Association (BIBA) (`www.backgammon-biba.co.uk`), run by Michael and Sharen Crane, does a tremendous job in promoting the game and runs tournaments throughout the year with reasonable entry fees. They also maintain details on clubs in the UK.

Gammon Village

Online backgammon magazines have come and gone but Gammon Village, `www.gammonvillage.com`, has stayed the course. This magazine is a cut above the rest, providing an impressive list of contributors and columnists. An annual subscription of $50 is charged but that's an absolute bargain for the wealth of material that you gain access to. The lessons provided by the columnists are of a very high quality indeed.

Backgammon Galore

Tom Keith's excellent 'Backgammon Galore!' site is at `www.bkgm.com`. Tom is a long-time backgammon enthusiast and his site reflects his love of the game. It covers a wide range of backgammon information including reviews of every backgammon book ever published.

Index

BUSINESS, CAREERS & PERSONAL FINANCE

Accounting For Dummies, 4th Edition*
978-0-470-24600-9

Bookkeeping Workbook For Dummies†
978-0-470-16983-4

Commodities For Dummies
978-0-470-04928-0

Doing Business in China For Dummies
978-0-470-04929-7

E-Mail Marketing For Dummies
978-0-470-19087-6

Job Interviews For Dummies, 3rd Edition*†
978-0-470-17748-8

Personal Finance Workbook For Dummies*†
978-0-470-09933-9

Real Estate License Exams For Dummies
978-0-7645-7623-2

Six Sigma For Dummies
978-0-7645-6798-8

Small Business Kit For Dummies, 2nd Edition*†
978-0-7645-5984-6

Telephone Sales For Dummies
978-0-470-16836-3

BUSINESS PRODUCTIVITY & MICROSOFT OFFICE

Access 2007 For Dummies
978-0-470-03649-5

Excel 2007 For Dummies
978-0-470-03737-9

Office 2007 For Dummies
978-0-470-00923-9

Outlook 2007 For Dummies
978-0-470-03830-7

PowerPoint 2007 For Dummies
978-0-470-04059-1

Project 2007 For Dummies
978-0-470-03651-8

QuickBooks 2008 For Dummies
978-0-470-18470-7

Quicken 2008 For Dummies
978-0-470-17473-9

Salesforce.com For Dummies, 2nd Edition
978-0-470-04893-1

Word 2007 For Dummies
978-0-470-03658-7

EDUCATION, HISTORY, REFERENCE & TEST PREPARATION

African American History For Dummies
978-0-7645-5469-8

Algebra For Dummies
978-0-7645-5325-7

Algebra Workbook For Dummies
978-0-7645-8467-1

Art History For Dummies
978-0-470-09910-0

ASVAB For Dummies, 2nd Edition
978-0-470-10671-6

British Military History For Dummies
978-0-470-03213-8

Calculus For Dummies
978-0-7645-2498-1

Canadian History For Dummies, 2nd Edition
978-0-470-83656-9

Geometry Workbook For Dummies
978-0-471-79940-5

The SAT I For Dummies, 6th Edition
978-0-7645-7193-0

Series 7 Exam For Dummies
978-0-470-09932-2

World History For Dummies
978-0-7645-5242-7

FOOD, GARDEN, HOBBIES & HOME

Bridge For Dummies, 2nd Edition
978-0-471-92426-5

Coin Collecting For Dummies, 2nd Edition
978-0-470-22275-1

Cooking Basics For Dummies, 3rd Edition
978-0-7645-7206-7

Drawing For Dummies
978-0-7645-5476-6

Etiquette For Dummies, 2nd Edition
978-0-470-10672-3

Gardening Basics For Dummies*†
978-0-470-03749-2

Knitting Patterns For Dummies
978-0-470-04556-5

Living Gluten-Free For Dummies†
978-0-471-77383-2

Painting Do-It-Yourself For Dummies
978-0-470-17533-0

HEALTH, SELF HELP, PARENTING & PETS

Anger Management For Dummies
978-0-470-03715-7

Anxiety & Depression Workbook For Dummies
978-0-7645-9793-0

Dieting For Dummies, 2nd Edition
978-0-7645-4149-0

Dog Training For Dummies, 2nd Edition
978-0-7645-8418-3

Horseback Riding For Dummies
978-0-470-09719-9

Infertility For Dummies†
978-0-470-11518-3

Meditation For Dummies with CD-ROM, 2nd Edition
978-0-471-77774-8

Post-Traumatic Stress Disorder For Dummies
978-0-470-04922-8

Puppies For Dummies, 2nd Edition
978-0-470-03717-1

Thyroid For Dummies, 2nd Edition†
978-0-471-78755-6

Type 1 Diabetes For Dummies*†
978-0-470-17811-9

* Separate Canadian edition also available
† Separate U.K. edition also available

INTERNET & DIGITAL MEDIA

AdWords For Dummies
978-0-470-15252-2

Blogging For Dummies, 2nd Edition
978-0-470-23017-6

**Digital Photography All-in-One
Desk Reference For Dummies, 3rd Edition**
978-0-470-03743-0

Digital Photography For Dummies, 5th Edition
978-0-7645-9802-9

**Digital SLR Cameras & Photography
For Dummies, 2nd Edition**
978-0-470-14927-0

**eBay Business All-in-One Desk Reference
For Dummies**
978-0-7645-8438-1

eBay For Dummies, 5th Edition*
978-0-470-04529-9

eBay Listings That Sell For Dummies
978-0-471-78912-3

Facebook For Dummies
978-0-470-26273-3

The Internet For Dummies, 11th Edition
978-0-470-12174-0

Investing Online For Dummies, 5th Edition
978-0-7645-8456-5

iPod & iTunes For Dummies, 5th Edition
978-0-470-17474-6

MySpace For Dummies
978-0-470-09529-4

Podcasting For Dummies
978-0-471-74898-4

**Search Engine Optimization
For Dummies, 2nd Edition**
978-0-471-97998-2

Second Life For Dummies
978-0-470-18025-9

**Starting an eBay Business For Dummies,
3rd Edition†**
978-0-470-14924-9

GRAPHICS, DESIGN & WEB DEVELOPMENT

**Adobe Creative Suite 3 Design Premium
All-in-One Desk Reference For Dummies**
978-0-470-11724-8

**Adobe Web Suite CS3 All-in-One Desk
Reference For Dummies**
978-0-470-12099-6

AutoCAD 2008 For Dummies
978-0-470-11650-0

**Building a Web Site For Dummies,
3rd Edition**
978-0-470-14928-7

**Creating Web Pages All-in-One Desk
Reference For Dummies, 3rd Edition**
978-0-470-09629-1

**Creating Web Pages For Dummies,
8th Edition**
978-0-470-08030-6

Dreamweaver CS3 For Dummies
978-0-470-11490-2

Flash CS3 For Dummies
978-0-470-12100-9

Google SketchUp For Dummies
978-0-470-13744-4

InDesign CS3 For Dummies
978-0-470-11865-8

**Photoshop CS3 All-in-One
Desk Reference For Dummies**
978-0-470-11195-6

Photoshop CS3 For Dummies
978-0-470-11193-2

Photoshop Elements 5 For Dummies
978-0-470-09810-3

SolidWorks For Dummies
978-0-7645-9555-4

Visio 2007 For Dummies
978-0-470-08983-5

Web Design For Dummies, 2nd Edition
978-0-471-78117-2

Web Sites Do-It-Yourself For Dummies
978-0-470-16903-2

Web Stores Do-It-Yourself For Dummies
978-0-470-17443-2

LANGUAGES, RELIGION & SPIRITUALITY

Arabic For Dummies
978-0-471-77270-5

Chinese For Dummies, Audio Set
978-0-470-12766-7

French For Dummies
978-0-7645-5193-2

German For Dummies
978-0-7645-5195-6

Hebrew For Dummies
978-0-7645-5489-6

Ingles Para Dummies
978-0-7645-5427-8

Italian For Dummies, Audio Set
978-0-470-09586-7

Italian Verbs For Dummies
978-0-471-77389-4

Japanese For Dummies
978-0-7645-5429-2

Latin For Dummies
978-0-7645-5431-5

Portuguese For Dummies
978-0-471-78738-9

Russian For Dummies
978-0-471-78001-4

Spanish Phrases For Dummies
978-0-7645-7204-3

Spanish For Dummies
978-0-7645-5194-9

Spanish For Dummies, Audio Set
978-0-470-09585-0

The Bible For Dummies
978-0-7645-5296-0

Catholicism For Dummies
978-0-7645-5391-2

The Historical Jesus For Dummies
978-0-470-16785-4

Islam For Dummies
978-0-7645-5503-9

**Spirituality For Dummies,
2nd Edition**
978-0-470-19142-2

NETWORKING AND PROGRAMMING

ASP.NET 3.5 For Dummies
978-0-470-19592-5

C# 2008 For Dummies
978-0-470-19109-5

Hacking For Dummies, 2nd Edition
978-0-470-05235-8

Home Networking For Dummies, 4th Edition
978-0-470-11806-1

Java For Dummies, 4th Edition
978-0-470-08716-9

**Microsoft® SQL Server™ 2008 All-in-One
Desk Reference For Dummies**
978-0-470-17954-3

**Networking All-in-One Desk Reference
For Dummies, 2nd Edition**
978-0-7645-9939-2

**Networking For Dummies,
8th Edition**
978-0-470-05620-2

SharePoint 2007 For Dummies
978-0-470-09941-4

**Wireless Home Networking
For Dummies, 2nd Edition**
978-0-471-74940-0

OPERATING SYSTEMS & COMPUTER BASICS

iMac For Dummies, 5th Edition
978-0-7645-8458-9

Laptops For Dummies, 2nd Edition
978-0-470-05432-1

Linux For Dummies, 8th Edition
978-0-470-11649-4

MacBook For Dummies
978-0-470-04859-7

**Mac OS X Leopard All-in-One
Desk Reference For Dummies**
978-0-470-05434-5

Mac OS X Leopard For Dummies
978-0-470-05433-8

Macs For Dummies, 9th Edition
978-0-470-04849-8

PCs For Dummies, 11th Edition
978-0-470-13728-4

Windows® Home Server For Dummies
978-0-470-18592-6

Windows Server 2008 For Dummies
978-0-470-18043-3

**Windows Vista All-in-One
Desk Reference For Dummies**
978-0-471-74941-7

Windows Vista For Dummies
978-0-471-75421-3

Windows Vista Security For Dummies
978-0-470-11805-4

SPORTS, FITNESS & MUSIC

Coaching Hockey For Dummies
978-0-470-83685-9

Coaching Soccer For Dummies
978-0-471-77381-8

Fitness For Dummies, 3rd Edition
978-0-7645-7851-9

Football For Dummies, 3rd Edition
978-0-470-12536-6

GarageBand For Dummies
978-0-7645-7323-1

Golf For Dummies, 3rd Edition
978-0-471-76871-5

Guitar For Dummies, 2nd Edition
978-0-7645-9904-0

**Home Recording For Musicians
For Dummies, 2nd Edition**
978-0-7645-8884-6

**iPod & iTunes For Dummies,
5th Edition**
978-0-470-17474-6

Music Theory For Dummies
978-0-7645-7838-0

Stretching For Dummies
978-0-470-06741-3

Get smart @ dummies.com®

- Find a full list of Dummies titles
- Look into loads of FREE on-site articles
- Sign up for FREE eTips e-mailed to you weekly
- See what other products carry the Dummies name
- Shop directly from the Dummies bookstore
- Enter to win new prizes every month!

Printed and bound by CPI Group (UK) Ltd, Croydon, CR0 4YY